Acquisition and transfer of property in Islamic law

Malthouse Law Books

Abdulrazaq, M. T., *Nigerian Revenue Law*
Abiola Sanni, *An Introduction to Nigerian Business Law*
Adah C. E., *The Nigerian Law of Evidence*
Asuzu, C., *Fair hearing in Nigeria*
Bambale, Y. Y., *Crimes and Punishment under Islamic Law*
Bambale, Y. Y., *An Outline of Islamic Jurisprudence*
Bambale, Y. Y., *Islamic Law Relating to Property and Commercial Transaction*
Emiri, F., *The Law of Restitution in Nigeria*
Fogam, P., *Law of Contract*
Goldface-Irokalibe, I.J., *The Law of Banking in Nigeria*
Ikoni, U.D., *An Introduction to Nigerian Environmental Law*
Ladan, M.T., *Introduction to jurisprudence: classical and Islamic*
Mowoe, Yinka, *Constitutional Law in Nigeria Vol. I*
Olong, Adefi M., *Administrative Law in Nigeria: an introduction*
Olong, Adefi M., *The Nigerian legal system: an introduction*
Omorogbe, Yinka, *Oil and Gas Law in Nigeria*
Omotesho, Aboaba, *The Law of Tort in Nigeria: selected themes*
Sagay, I., *Nigerian Family Law: Principles, Cases, Statutes and Commentaries*
Sagay, I., *Law of Succession in Nigeria: Principles, Cases, Statutes and Commentaries*
Utuama, A. A., *The Law of Trust and their Uses in Nigeria*
Utuama, A. A., *Planning Law in Nigeria*
Uvieghara E. E., *Labour Law in Nigeria*
Uvieghara E. E., *Sale of Goods*
Yakubu J. A., *Limits to the Application of Foreign Laws*
Yakubu J. A., *Harmonisation of Laws in Africa*
Yakubu J. A., *International Contracts: Evolution and Theory*
Yakubu J. A., *Law of contract in Nigeria*
Yakubu J. A., *Press Law in Nigeria*
Yakubu J. A., *Administration of Justice in Nigeria*
Yakubu J. A. and Oyewo A. T., *Criminal Law and Procedure in Nigeria*

Acquisition and transfer of property in Islamic law

Yahaya Yunusa Bambale
LLB, LLM, Ph.D (ABU) BL
Ahmadu Bello University
Zaria, Nigeria

malthouse MP

Malthouse Press Limited

Lagos, Benin, Ibadan, Jos, Port-Harcourt, Zaria

Malthouse Press Limited
43 Onitana Street, Off Stadium Hotel Road,
Surulere, Lagos, Lagos State
E-mail: malthouse_press@yahoo.com
malthouse_lagos@yahoo.co.uk
Tel: +234 (01) -773 53 44; 0802 364 2402

First Published 2007
ISBN 978 023 248 6

Distributors:

African Books Collective
Oxford, United Kingdom
Email: abc@africanbookscollective.com
Website: http://www.africanbookscollective.com

Dedication

This book is dedicated to the Economic and Financial Crimes Commission for its fight to rid the Nigerian Society of corruption and corrupt practices.

Foreword

I have had the advantage of reading in draft the book titled: *Acquisition & Transfer of Property in Islamic Law,* ably authored by Dr. Y. Y. Bambale of the Department of Islamic Law, Faculty of Law, Ahmadu Bello University (ABU) Zaria. The book is essentially on mode of acquisition and transfer of private property in Islamic law. I think this is the first of its kind, generally on the law of property in Islamic law authored by a Nigerian. The author has painstakingly dissected the various definitions accorded by jurists to the word *Milk*. He differentiated the word from possession, though in Islamic Law generally, hardly does one note any remarkable difference in usage of the two terms. Rights of ownership and transfer of property are lawful as sanctioned by Islam. This includes all methods of acquisitions short of extortion, oppression, fraud, *et cetera*. It is a fundamental right in Islam. Except in circumstances where the law for some obvious reasons can deprive a person from ownership or its transfer, every individual has right to the enjoyment including transfer of his property without any hindrance. Indeed one can legally acquire land through inheritance, purchase, reviving of a vacant land, grant, loan, *et cetera*. Land can also be held in trust by the authority on behalf of the community (*harim*) (allodial ownership). In fact one can acquire land through the illegal means such as *ghasb* (usurpation), although strictly prohibited. One the other hand, one can transfer property through, sale, gift, loan, pledge, etc. in Islamic law. It can thus be seen that Islamic Law explicitly recognizes the right of individuals to acquire and dispose of properties in a legal manner. What Islamic law frowns at seriously is acquisition through the illegal forms. It also frowns at land speculation. No land should be left to fallow for more than three years. The Amir (leader) should re-allocate a land left to fallow without justifiable cause(s) above that period. This was the practice during the period of Caliph Umar bn Al-khattab. The author discusses the modes of ownership among which is the public ownership along with general exceptions to it. It indeed promotes principle of public good within the society. For instance, no individual should be allowed by the law to have monopoly over minerals such as gold, silver, iron, coal, petroleum, kerosene, copper etc including water and salt. Respect for labour in order for a Muslim to acquire means of sustenance legally has a special position in Islam. No one is encouraged to become lazy or a burden on another. The author narrates to us the experiences of the Prophet (SAW) as a shepherd and of his *Sahaba* and many other prophets who had visible and dignified professions upon which they relied for sustenance. This must serve as a pointer to the generality of the Muslim *Ummah* to condemn in no uncertain terms and discourage the laissez-faire attitude to labour or gainful employment embarked upon by some of its members. It is shameful for one, except in absolute necessity, to be a burden upon another. After all, there are trades, vocations, professions, too numerous to mention. It is this apathy that makes the author to observe:

> Looking at the trend today, Muslims are really lagging in the field of science and technology,

This observation is very apt. It was rightly done in my view. The Muslims must awake from their slumber and throw away the yokes of passivity, laziness and naivety. No one can help a man better than himself.

The author discusses the relationship that should exist between the employers and the employees. Each of the two needs to know the Extent of his rights and limitations. You will need to acquaint yourself with these mutual rights, obligations, duties, limitations etc.

If you are the type destined to take to sales and purchases, the author has considered these in this Chapter 3.

Is there any difference between a gift and a *Sadaqah* (charitable transfer of a thing with a view to getting reward from Allah)? This is the topic of Chapter 4 of this book. It is mandatory to read as we all make out gifts and *Sadaqah*. We sometime contemplate on revoking a gift. Can one really do so? I recommend this chapter of this book for your study. Chapters 5 and 6 discuss the testate and intestate successions. Testate succession ordinarily refers to the making of a will. Can a Muslim make a will? To whom? Is a will revocable? What are conditions for a valid will? Chapter 5 answers this question. It is necessary to read this chapter to avoid the confusion often created by some people between a gift *inter vivoce* and a *Wasiyya* (bequest). You must as well read chapter 6 as you must one day be involved in distribution of an estate left by a deceased person whether related on any of the grounds which qualify one to inherit or as torch bearer of the society as a learned person, Judge or community leader. You cannot distribute a *tarikah* and what it entails if you do not possess the requisite knowledge to do so. It is therefore a must.

In conclusion, I commend the effort of the author for his articulation on the topics treated by his book. We must pray for more of his type. The truth is that unless those who know write, those who do not know shall continue to grope in the darkness. Allah the high has placed the responsibility upon the learned to educate the ignorant. May Allah reward the author abundantly and may we be blessed to borrow a leaf from Mallam (Dr) Bambale.

Hon. Justice (Dr.) Ibrahim Tanko Muhammad
Justice's Chambers
Supreme Court
Abuja

Preface

The larger portion of the Muslims in our society, hardly know how to differentiate between lawful and unlawful means of acquiring and transferring ownership of property. Even, where they do, they care little or none to differentiate in practice between the two. Greed, corruption, embezzlement, criminal breach of trust, '419' syndicates and other like vices have taken the place of the lawful ways of acquiring property. It is in view of this that the writing of this book is handy. It intends to explore, analyse and present the nature and extent of Islamic law relating to acquisition and transferring of ownership of property. The end result of doing so will be of benefit to the generality of Muslims toward changing their attitudes in acquiring and transferring ownership of property lawfully in accordance with tenets of the Sharia. Also, it is to serve as a reference material for the use of the public, academicians, judges, students, etc. in tackling the problems relating to acquisition and transferring ownership of property.

Finally, the book seeks to introduce the readers to the basic principles of the Islamic Law relating to ownership of property, how best to acquire and transfer it. This is by no means a comprehensive study as some points of law have been omitted. The vacuum can best be filled by reference to the original sources.

Chapter one comprises the concept of ownership, types, rules and modes relating to acquisition of property. It also discusses the lawful and unlawful means of acquisition, property. It also discusses the lawful and unlawful means of acquisition, property and its classification.

Chapter two discusses work especially with ones hands as the best and most dignified way of earning a living. The various types of work ranging from manual or physical to professional, intellectual and salaried employment are discussed. The chapter enunciated the qualities of a good worker, his rights and how to protect such worker and the question of unemployment generally.

In chapter three, the most frequent mode of acquisition and transfer of ownership i.e. sale, is discussed. The constituents of a valid sale, conduct of parties in a sale transaction, the lawful and unlawful sale transactions are also discussed.

Chapter four borders on gift and how it is distinguished from related concepts like Sadaqah, Ariya, etc. It also discusses the conditions for a valid gift structure, and how it can be revoked.

Chapter five is a discussion on testate succession i.e. will and the types, object and form of a will. Also discussed is the testator, beneficiary, subject matter of a will, revocation of a will and when it is said to have lapsed.

Chapter six is a discussion on intestate succession. A brief discourse on pre-Islamic form of succession is made. Also discussed are the constituents of succession, grounds of such succession, liabilities of the deceased person, and the fractions in succession, etc.

The last chapter is an exposition on the legal impediments to the acquisition or transfer of ownership of property. Fraud, hoarding, bribery, death, sickness, gift, theft, etc. are impairing factors to the acquisition or transfer of property ownership generally. This book is an attempt in the direction of distinguishing the lawful from the unlawful means of acquisition and transfer of property in Islamic Law.

Contents

Abbreviations

D - Daughter
F - Father
GB - Gername Brother(s)
GS - Gername Sister(s)
HHS - How High Soever
HLS - How Low Soever
LCM - Lowest Common Multiple
M - Mother
P - Praepositus (deceased)
PBUH - Peace Be Upon Him
R - Residue
SAW - Sallallahu alaihi Wasallam (May the blessing and peace of Allah be upon Him)
W - Wife

Chapter 1

Concept of ownership

The concept of ownership has been variously defined by different writers, Muslims and non-Muslims alike.

Among the definitions by non-Muslim is that of Sir John Salmond who states that:

> Ownership of a material thing is nothing more than a figurative substitute for the ownership of a particular kind of right in respect of that thing.[1]

Another definition looks at it not as a particular kind of right, but as the "bundle of rights.[2] But, Sir Austin defines it as:

> a right indefinite in point of user, unrestricted in point of disposition and unlimited in point of duration.[3]

These definitions seem restrictive and limited as far as modern law[4] is concerned because they apply to fewer things as the complexity of social life and the interference of the state with the individual increases.[5]

A better and wider definition of ownership is the one given by Sir

---

[1] *Jurisprudence* (8th edition) p.279; of, now 12th edition.

[2] Markby (n.d) *Element of law*, p. 309.

[3] See, Austin (n.d) *Second Book of Jurisprudence*. P. 477.

[4] See, Goodhart (1930), *Essays in Jurisprudence and the Common Law*, p. 41.

[5] Tyler, E.L.G. and Palmer, N.E (1973) *On Crossley Vaines' Personal Property:* 5th ed., Butterworth, p.39.

Frederick Pollock as:

> ...the entirety of the powers of use and disposal allowed by the law.[6]

But, in the context of the Nigeria customary law, the idea of ownership as in the English law is unknown, because of the controversy surrounding whether property - i.e. land - in African communities can be said to be 'owned'.

This is based on the practice that one can obtain ownership of a property and have the possession of such property but cannot have the power to alienate the same.

That is why Dr. Coker[7] has submitted that the greatest right which a person can have in property - i.e. land - is the right of possession and not 'ownership'.

Therefore, whatever definition is to be given to ownership must be in reference to possession and power of alienation.

The Arabic word *milk* is translated as ownership, even though *milk* covers a wider area than ownership in the English sense because it includes not only the physical objects, but, also, proprietary rights like the right of pre-emption.

In this book for the sake of convenience, the word ownership is adapted as the nearest English equivalent of *milk.*

Ownership is defined as:

> The expression of the connection existing between an individual and a thing which is under his absolute power and control to the exclusion of control and disposition by others.[8]

It is also defined as a legal order of the Islamic state regarding the possession or use of any property.[9] Any individual receiving this legal order of the Islamic state becomes the rightful owner of that property. This definition is restrictive because it refers to land only.

From the above definitions, the concept of ownership in Islamic law

---

[6] See, Pollock F., (n.d), *First Book of Jurisprudence* p. 179

[7] See Coker (1958); *Family Property Among the Yorubas,*, London ; pp. 32-4.

[8] Naseef, A.O. (1982), *Encyclopaedia of Seerah*; The Muslims School Trust, vol. II, p. 365.

[9] Ibid.

is comprehensive in the sense that it does not only encompass the possession of the property owned, but all the property rights associated with it.

Possession (or *Qabd* in Arabic) is an important element or attribute of ownership. It is also a means of acquiring ownership to the extent that one in de facto possession can assert ownership to all with the exception of the real owner. Possession is then the overt use of the benefits of the property. Possession in Islamic law may be actual (*Haqiqi*) or symbolical (*Hukmi*). Possession is said to be *actual* as when a man grasps a thing in his hands or puts it in his pocket like money. But, it is not possible with things like land, house, ship, table or chair. Possession in such cases is then symbolical (*Hukmi*).[10]
What is necessary to constitute possession is the intention to exclude other persons coupled with the power to carry it out.

Therefore, when all but the owner or his servants or agents are totally excluded and no other person has a right to possession of the thing at the time, it is then known as *complete possession.* It is *incomplete*, where one out of more than one owner of an undivided share (*Musha'*) has a right to possession over every particle of the property as the other co-owner(s).[11]

The right of ownership of property has been sanctioned by Islam; which includes all lawful ways of gaining it without resort to oppression, extortion or fraud, etc. It is a social principle of Islam, that there is absolute equality in everything relating to the individual except in the ability for work and effort. This distinction is even acknowledged by the Holy Qur'an thus:

> And for men is the benefit of what they earn. And for women is the benefit of what they earn.[12]

From these, it can be deduced that the Holy Qur'an and the *Sunnah* very explicitly recognize the right of individuals to acquire ownership of property and to dispose of it in a legal manner. Other rights, such as the right to the safety of the property from theft, dacoity, deceit, etc., follow.

---

[10] Qadri A.A., (1986) *Islamic Jurisprudence in the Modern World;* Taj Company, Delhi ; p. 365

[11] See generally, Abdul Rahim. M.A., (1978); *The Principles of Muhammadan Jurisprudence:* All Pakistan Legal Decisions, Lahore; pp. 275-279.

[12] Holy Qur'an, Ch.4 V.32.

Those who endanger the safety of the property and do not honour the right to ownership are severely punished as stated in the following Quranic verse:

> As to the thief, male or female, cut off his or her hands: a punishment by way of example, from God, for their crime and God is exalted in power.[13]

Classification of ownership

Ownership of property is classified into three namely:

Absolute or permanent ownership

The Holy Qur'an says:

> To God belongeth the dominion of the heavens and the earth; and God hath power over all things[14]

This shows man is simply the vicegerent of Allah on earth. For an individual to have permanent ownership is not acceptable to reason on the ground that life itself is not permanent. Permanent ownership is, therefore, reserved for Allah alone, as explained thus:

> To Him belongs the dominion of the Heaven and the earth in the end, it is to Him, that ye shall be brought back.[15]

Islam regards the owner of property as one who holds the property on behalf of the community in the capacity of a *trustee:* or a representative and not by his having absolute right of ownership. In short, absolute or

---

[13] Ch. 5 V. 41.
[14] Ch. 3 V. 189.
[15] Ch. 49 V. 44.

permanent ownership of all things (property included) belongs to none but Allah.[16]

Public ownership

In Islamic law, public ownership simply means that all property and wealth belongs to the community which grants rights of ownership or benefits of different things to its citizen. Some of the things of common utility are kept in the custody of the community, while other things are given to individuals.

The division between the things that belong to the community and those that belong to the individuals is entirely based on the common good of society.

Thus, Islamic law recognizes the basic right of the individual to own property, but at the same time, it specifies certain things it considered not allowed for individual ownership. So, that, no individual, single or in association with others, may possess them or manage them or monopolize them for his personal benefit against the common good.

All such properties are declared as public property and this is deduced from the sayings of the Holy Prophet (S.A.W). Ubyaz bin Hamal said:

> I went to the Holy Prophet (S.A.W.) and asked for the grant of salty water in Marb. He agreed, but one of those present said, 'O Messenger of God, why are you entrusting him the treasure of salt? After knowing the facts of the case, the Holy Prophet (S.A.W) refused to grant me that salty water.[17]

From this *Hadith*, jurists decided that all kinds of minerals e.g. gold, silver, iron, coal, petroleum, kerosene, copper etc. should be public property and no individual should own them for his personal benefit only.

In conclusion, as a general rule, private ownership is allowed, while public ownership is an exception and adopts it merely to limit the right

---

[16] Khan, M.M (1976), *Sahih al-Bukhari*, Hilal Yayinlari, Ankara-Turkey, Vol. 3, p. 379.

[17] Ibid., p. 380

to property, so that it does not grow to such an extent as to endanger the good of society. This shows that articles of necessity which are used by a very large section of the community or projects of great common value - e.g. public works, railways, post office, currency, hydro-electricity projects, etc. - should be owned and managed by the state for the benefit of the community and cannot be entrusted to private ownership.

Private ownership

Islamic law recognises the right of private ownership through legal possession of all types of property but does not leave the individual entirely free to use the right in any way he likes. It shows that private ownership is allowed in principle, but is subject to such limitations as will render it harmless. Hence, unlawful ways of obtaining it by resorting to oppression, extortion, fraud, theft, robbery, usurpation, misappropriation, gambling, etc., denounced in unequivocal terms, as the following Qur'anic verses and prophetic traditions shows:

> 1. And swallow not up your property among yourselves by false means.[18]
>
> 2. As to the thief, male or female, cut off his or her hands: a punishment by way of example, from God, for their crimes: and God is exalted in power.[19]

The Holy Prophet (S.A.W) condemned those who usurp other people's property by false pretences in these words:

> Whoever usurps even a small part of the land (or property) of another will be made to wear the same as a collar (of fire) on his neck (on the day of judgement).[20]

---

[18] Ch.2 V.188

[19] Ch. 5 V. 38.

[20] Siddiqi, A. H. (1976), *Sahih Muslim,* Dar al-Arabia, Beirut, Lebanon, Vol. III, p. 1054.

Also, the Holy Prophet (S.A.W) warns people against transgressing on the property of other thus:

> And he who seizes another Muslim's money illegally will be exposed in the hereafter to Allah's wrath.[21]

The importance of authorizing and allowing the community to enact the necessary legislation to organise private ownership and to change it whenever the public interest demands it, cannot be over-emphasized.

Apart from the limitations above, the right of private ownership is attested to by the Holy Qur'an when it stated thus:

> And for men is the benefit of what they earn. And for women is the benefit of what they earn.[22]

And it is further strengthened by the Holy Prophet (S.A.W,) when he said that:

> Anyone who died while protecting his property is a Martyr.[23]

Rules relating to acquisition of private ownership

The general rule is that absolute ownership belongs to Allah alone and man is simply the vicegerent of Allah on earth. What is allowed here as it concerns individual, is the *legal ownership* - i.e. the right of possession, enjoyment and transfer of the property.

Based upon this, the rules governing private ownership are thus:[24]

1. The first and foremost rule is that any one who acquires ownership of a property, should continue to utilise the property at all times for his own use and benefit in a rightful way as well as for the community. The Holy Prophet (S.A.W) is reported to have said

---

[21] Khan, M. M. (1976), ibid., vol. 3, p. 380.

[22] Ch. 4 v. 32.

[23] Siddiqi, A.H. (1976), ibid., Vol. III, p. 1054.

[24] Manan, M.A. (1970); *Islamic Economic Theory and Practice*; Delhi (India), pp.89-98.

that:

> The person who seizes land belonging to nobody would cease to have any right to such land if he did not reasonably exploit it after 3 years of possession.[25]

This right of private ownership was reiterated and enforced by Caliph Umar, who is said to have taken back some of the lands given to Bilal ibn al-Harith simply on the ground that he (Bilal) did not utilise all the lands given to him by the Holy Prophet (S.A.W). In short, non-use of property is not allowed in Islamic Law.

2. The second rule is that, the owner of private property must pay the *zakat* (alms due) in proportion to the property owned. It is to be paid out of all kinds of property lawfully owned, such as gold, silver, currency of any kind, agricultural produce, animals, etc. It is paid if the property owned is with the owner for a complete one year and it has reaches the *nisab* - i.e. the minimum amount for which *zakat* is payable. The essence of the payment here, cannot be over-emphasized as it bridges the gap or inequality between the rich and the poor; bringing about peace and harmony in the community.

3. The third rule, in regard to the conduct of the owner of private property is that he must make beneficial use of the property 'in a gratuitous way,' which in effect means using it in the proper way beneficial to the community as a whole and conducive to its prosperity and welfare.

   It is stated in the Holy Qur'an that:

   > The parable of those who spend their substance in the way of God is that of a grain of corn: it groweth seven ears, and each ear hath a hundred grains. God giveth manifold increase to whom He pleaseth: And God careth for all and He knoweth all things.[26]

   The reason for this can be seen in a situation where, due to

---

[25] Imam Malik (1982), *Al-Muwatta*; Diwan Press , England , p. 346.

[26] Ch.2 V. 261.

complexity of modern life, *zakat* cannot meet all the requirements of the society, as it used to be during the time of the Holy prophet (S.A.W.) and immediately after Him. Hence, the utilization of property 'in the way of Allah' is highly significant, because it is only through such, the Muslim community can prosper.

4. The fourth rule, is that the owner of the property, even though he is to use it in a beneficial way. Yet, it is imposed upon him as a duty not to use it in way as to cause harm to others or the community at large. Where harm is done to others when using it, will amount to aggression which is highly forbidden from what the Holy Qur'an says:

    > And fight in the way of God those who fight against you, but be not aggressive surely, Allah loves not the aggressors.[27]

    In this connection, Abu Huraira reported that the Holy Prophet (S.A.W.) said:

    > Excess of water should not be withheld, arresting thereby the growth of herbage.[28]

    But, this modern trend is that ownership of property especially wealth is concentrated in a few hands, hence defeating in very essence of the maxim:

    > No harm is allowed whether the doer benefits from it or not,[29]

    which is a saying of the Holy Prophet (S.A.W.).
5. The fifth rule is that ownership of property should be acquired by lawful means, because acquiring it unlawful destroys people in the end. It is contained in the Holy Qur'an that:

    > O ye who believe, Eat not up your property among

---

[27] Ch.2 V. 190

[28] Imam Malik (1982), Ibid., p. 346.

[29] As quoted by Higab M. (1983) *Islam is the all Divine Messages in one*, Vol. 1, I.P.B., Lagos, Nigeria; p. 185.

> yourselves in vanities, but let there be amongst you traffic and trade by mutual good-will, nor kill (or destroy) yourselves: for verily God hath been to you most merciful.[30]

To this end, hoarding, monopoly, dishonesty, bribery and all illegal ways of acquiring property are denounced and should be suppressed in the interest of the community.

6. The sixth rule, being that the owner of private property should use it in a balanced way, so that he may not be prodigal or parsimonious in its use. The Holy Qur'an says:

> Make not thy hand tied (like a niggard's) to thy neck nor stretch it forth to its utmost reach so that thou become blameworthy and destitute.[31]

One is deemed prodigal, when he wastes the property through neglect likened to a case of a person who lacks financial wisdom. On the other hand, one is parsimonious as regards the use of property when he holds it back denying people its benefit. Indeed, one who indulges himself in such an act renders him progressively poorer in the true sense of the term inasmuch as he stultifies his faculties, and by putting that which he possesses out of service and out of circulation, renders it completely barren and unfruitful.

7. The seventh rule, is that by the use of the property owned, it should secure for the owner due benefits. It will be undue benefits himself only, politically, economically, etc. This, indeed, neglects the spirit of Islam, if one uses the property for the attainment of such selfish objectives.

8. The last and the eight rules, is that one who acquires ownership of property should use it in the best interest of his living, by effecting its proper control and distribution. But, after his death, the ownership of property will best be put in proper control and distribution in the interest of living by the rightful application of the

[30] Ch.4 V.29.

[31] Ch.17 V.29.

Islamic law of inheritance.

The mode of acquiring ownership of property

Acquisition of property by the individual (male or female) is recognized by Islam. There is no limitation placed upon the property or wealth which an individual may acquire or give away. This is indeed opposed to communism or socialism on the one hand and capitalism on the other hand. In short, in its form it is neither communism or socialism nor capitalism. Despite the fact that an individual is free to acquire as much as he can, yet, the law tries its best to bring about a more or less equal distribution of wealth. An individual who acquires property is free, to dispose of the same, in the manner he so wishes as long as it is within the law. The only qualification is that he has to be very careful in his disposal of such property so that he does not waste it. There is a *Hadith* which says:

> Allah hates 3 things in you, unless talk and *wasting of wealth* and asking of begging frequently.[32]

Wealth here is referred to as the property of the individual as explained thus:

> There is no charity unless a man has sufficient to give, and he us himself in want or his family is in want or he has a debt to pay, it is more in the fitness of things that the debt should be paid than he should spend in charity or free a slave or make a gift; and such a gift or charity should be annulled, for he has no right to waste the wealth of the people (*ammalalonas*) and the Holy prophet (SAW) has said whoever takes the wealth of the people, that he may waste is, Allah will destroy his, unless he is a man well-known or his patience (*Sabr*) so that he prefers others before himself, though poverty, may afflict

[32] As quoted by Higab M. (1983), Ibid., p. 185.

him.[33]

The lawful ways of acquiring private ownership

The lawful ways of acquiring private ownership is as follows:

(a) The first and foremost means of obtaining or acquiring the right of (private) ownership is through the human of fort (work), and anyone who first takes possession (*Ihraz*) of a thing which is not the property of anyone else is considered to be the owner of that thing.[39] This is known as *original acquisition*. The Holy Prophet (SAW) is reported to have said:

> ...whoever cultivates land which is not the property of anyone has a better claim over it.[34]

(b) When there is the transfer of ownership from one to another (*Naql*) as in the case of sale and gift. This is in line with the view that 'everyone can make such dispositions of his *milk* property as he wishes, as long as the right of another is not attached or there is no excessive damage to another.'[35]

(c) When someone is made the successor of another - i.e. succession or inheritance (*khalf* or *waratha*).[36]

These are the ways of acquiring ownership of a private property allowed under Islamic law. But, at the same time, through the same means, it can also, be transferred.

---

[33] Karim, F.A. (1939), *Al-Hadis Mishkat-ul-Masabih*; The Book House, Lahore, Book II, p. 250.

[34] Imam Malik (1982), Ibid., p. 346.

[35] See generally, al-Mu-jallah Articles 1248-1250; Mohammed M.A.; (1973) *The Religion of Islam*, London, p. 280.

[36] Karim. F.A. (1939), ibid., Book II, p. 292

The unlawful ways of acquiring private ownership

All unlawful ways of acquiring property are denounced, which include stealing, robbery, gambling, misappropriation, lottery, hoarding, exploitation, usury, etc.[37]

For example, gambling is prohibited because it is a false or dishonest means of acquiring property. It includes all games and things in which the division of things and prizes is based not on any rational principles of rights or services but on some accidental or uncertain event.

Lottery, even of a small sum, promotes the habits of indolence, negation of honest labour, reducing some members of the society to penury, while others prosper at their expense.

Exploitation means one having a favour or taking undue advantage of the other partner to a transaction. It leads to ones destruction and it ruins the social order by turning it upside down. Hoarding is withholding the use of property in order to raise its prices artificially. Holy Prophet (SAW) forbids it when he said:

> ...whomever withholds (cereals or other articles of use to make them scarce and dear) is a sinner.[38]

The mentality of the hoarder is described in these words:

> He is a very bad man, who is grieved at low prices and pleased at high prices.[39]

Monopoly is the sole control of the supply of any property in the hands of one person or a group of persons who fires the price at a level most profitable to him or them, disregarding its benefit to the community. That is why the Holy Prophet (SAW) forbade private ownership or private control of things which are useful to the whole community.

---

[37] Higab, M. (1983), *Islam is the all Divine Messages in one*, vol. 1, I. P. B., Lagos, Nigeria, pp. 185 – 191.

[38] Karim. F.A. (1939), ibid., Book II, p.291.

[39] Ibid, Book II, p. 292.

Property and its classifications

Property (*Mal*) is defined as that which can e hoarded or secured for use and enjoyment at a time of need, or that to which man's desires incline and which man are in the habit of giving away to others and of excluding others there from.[40] This definition would have been better if it said that property is a physical object or what is connected with it, namely usufruct, in the shape of a product of a physical object.

'*Mal*' being the Arabic word for property is used in a much narrower sense, because it excludes things like the usufruct etc. Since 'property' is used in such wider sense, it is appropriate and can include all such, like the usufruct, disregarding the differences as to whether things or objects not having perceptible and tangible existence, are regarded as property or not.[41]

Some of the attributes of property are that; is must have some value i.e. it can be quantified in monetary terms. It must be a thing the use of which is permitted. It must be possessed and capable of being held in reserve.[42]

But this last attribute is added by the Hannafi School who did not regard the usufruct as property. In short, as far as the attributed of property are concerned; not all things can be regarded as property which is capable of being owned. For example, a corpse, wine, pig, light, air, sun, sea, fish while in the sea, etc.[43]

The classification of property can take the form of:

(a) *Movable (Manqul) and immovable (ghair manqul) property*. It is a movable property if it can be transferred from one place to another with case; while immovable property is such which can not be transported such as buildings and land, or which cannot be transferred to another place without damage or less such as trees before they have been uprooted or cut down.[44]

---

[40] Abdul Rahim, M. A. (1978), ibid., pp. 275-270.

[41] Ibid.

[42] Ibid.

[43] Ibid.

[44] Ibid.

(b) *Similar or fungibles (Mithli) and dissimilar or non-fungibles (Qimi)*

This classification pertains to movable property. An article or object is said to belong to the class of similar (*Mithli*) if the like of it can be had in the market. If such articles or objects are ordinarily sold by weight or measure; such as gold, silver, grain, oil, wheat, barley and the like. Conversely, things or articles such as land, houses, animals and the like are not ordinarily sold by weight or measure, are called dissimilar (*Qimi*).[45]

---

[45] Ibid.

Chapter 2

Work

The word 'work', 'labour' or 'services (are synonymous and often been confused). But, for the sake of this book, all, will be referring to one thing, because, the end result is the acquisition of ownership of whatever that may be involved, in form of property or proprietary rights.

Islam attaches great importance to work as a means of acquiring ownership of property. That is why it has been honoured and raised to the sacred standard of worship (*Ibadah*) in general, and *Jihad* (fighting in the cause of Allah) in particular.

The Holy Qur'an states that the Holy Prophet (SAW) should address the people thus:

> And say: work (righteousness): soon will God observe your work, and His Apostle.[1]

Also, Allah, the Exalted, Has said:

> And when the prayer is finished, then may ye disperse through the land and seek of the bounty of God.[2]

It was reported on good authority that some companions of the Holy Prophet (SAW) said, when they saw on one occasion a healthy and active youth hurrying to his work:

---

[1] Holy Qur'an, Ch. 9 v.105.

[2] Ch.62 v. 10.

> It would have been better for him if his youth, health, and activity have been spent in the way of Allah.
> Holy Prophet (SAW) said: 'Don't say this: If he has gone out to work to support his family, this will be in the way of Allah; if he has gone out to work to support his two old parents, this will be in the way of Allah; if he has gone out to work to support and protect himself, this will be in the way of Allah but if he has gone out to perform an act of boastfulness and ostentation, this will be in the way of Satan.' Also, that the Holy Prophet (SAW) said: 'One who works to support a widow or a poor man, is rewarded as if he were fighting in a holy war and as if he were fasting throughout the day and worshipping Allah all night long.[3]

The work contemplated here has to be a lawful one, so that where it is unlawful, whatever that is begotten out of it is also unlawful.

The Holy Prophet (SAW) has this to say:

> Flesh which is grown out of what is unlawful will not enter paradise, but hell is more fit for flesh which is grown out of what is unlawful.[4]

But, nowadays, people do not care the type of work they do so as long as they will get money, and do not bother themselves to find out whether it is obtained from a lawful source or not; and they consider this a kind of success.

The following incidents[5] will show a marked difference of the position of what is obtained lawfully and unlawfully between the early Muslims and Muslims nowadays:

> (1) It has been related that Abu Bakr had a slave who was working and brought his earnings to him

[3] Khan, M.M. (1976), *Sahih al-Bukhari;* Hilal Yayinlari, Ankara-Turkey, vol. 7; p. 202.

[4] Karim. F. A (1939), *Al-Hudis Mishkat-ul-Masabih*, The Book House, Lahore; Book II, p. 262.

[5] El-Geyoushi, M.I (n.d); *The meaning of Islam*, London Central Mosque, pp. 15-16.

and he used to eat some of the things that the slave brought to him. One day, the slave brought some milk. When Abubakar had drunk some of it, he asked the slave where he got this milk from. The slave replied 'I acted as a sorceror for a man in the pre-Islamic period, and not being good at it, I deceived him, but I met him and he gave me this milk, so that is what you have drunk. When, Abu Bakr heard this he put his fingers down his throat vomiting. He continued to do this until the people around thought that this would cause his death. After he had finished he supplicated God saying 'O God, I apologise to thee for what my veins have carried and mixed with the contents of my stomach.'

2) At one time, Caliph Umar had two sons who went with the Army and when the Army came back there was a lot of stuff which would be for Muslims. Umar's two sons, who were experienced in business, went to the chief of the Army and asked him to give them some money as loan to use for business and they would repay it when they reached home. The Army Chief loaned them the money and they sold the stuff and gained a lot of profit. When the news reached Umar, he asked 'Did the Army Chief give the same to all members of the Army, or only to you? His sons said, 'No, only to us? Umar's answer was 'you have no right to get this for he gave it to you because of your relationship to me and you have to repay it to the Muslims Treasury all that you have, both the income and the profit.'

(3) A man named Yunus Ibn Ubaid had a shop in which he sold certain kinds of garments. Some of these garments cost 400 dirhams and others cost 200 dirhams. Once, he went to pray at the

> mosque and left his nephew in the shop. A Bedouin came in to buy one of the garments which was for sale. The boy showed him one costing 200 dirhams and the man liked it and paid 400 dirhams for it and went away. On his way, he met Yunus. The man was carrying the garment on his arm and Yunus recognised it, and asked 'How much did you pay for it?.' The Bedouin said '400 dirhams, but Yunus said 'No, it does not cost more than 200.' Go back and return it.' The Bedouin said 'In my area it would cost 500' dirhams and I am pleased with it. But Yunus said, 'No, come with me, for the advice on religion is better than the world and what it gets? Then he took the man back with him and gave him back 200 dirhams and quarreled with his nephew saying 'Aren't you ashamed? Aren't you fearing God? Do you want to get 100% profit and do not give advice to a Muslim 'I swear by God I did not take it until he was pleased,' but Yunus said 'why did you accept for him what you do not accept for yourself?'

Not only is one expected to do a lawful work, he is to do it perfectly, by carrying out the responsibilities of his work. Where this is done it will only be equated and rewarded accordingly, just as a Muslim is rewarded in the Hereafter for worshipping Allah by performing prayer, fasting and the like. This is succinctly stated in the following tradition:

> The honest merchant will be a companion of the Holy Prophet (SAW), the righteous men, and the Martyrs in the other world.[6]

The Holy Prophet (SAW) exhorted Muslims to utilize the early morning in working and not to waste it in sleeping or idlying, as the early morning is the best time for fullest activity because in it man

---

[6] Transmitted by Al-Tirmidhi, as quoted by Qaradawi; (1984), *The Lawful and the Prohibited in Islam*, I.I.F.S.O.; p. 139.

enjoy a fresh energy after having a sufficient night's rests. In the Holy Qur'an, it is stated:

> And (have We not) created you in pairs, and made your sleep for rest and made the night as a covering and made the day as a means of subsistence?[7]

That is why Sakhr al-Ghamidi, one of the Holy Prophet's companions, on hearing the Prophet's exhortation, preferred to send his agents to trade for him in the early morning, and the result was that he made his fortune. Some companions of the Holy Prophet (SAW) even used to advice others not to sleep in the early morning since it is the time when the providence of Allah is distributed.

It is in this connection, the Holy Prophet (SAW) urged Muslims to work until the last moment of their lives or the last second in this world. This is explicit in the following tradition:

> If the hour came and one has in his hand a small palmshoot (i.e. he is about to plant it) and if he is able to plant it before raising himself up, then let them do so.[8]

Above all, looking at the essence of man's creation, one will see that he is expected to work hard for his livelihood:

> Verily, we have created man into toil and struggle.[9]

This is a challenge that man is destined to great heights but his advancement lies or is dependent on enduring hardship and perseverance. Man by nature is made to be able to bear all the difficulties and hardship in the struggle to achieve advancement, because he is created strong and physically able to withstand the hardships of life. This is referred to in the Holy Qur'an thus:

---

[7] Ch. 78 v. 8-11

[8] Al-Musnad; as quoted by Higab M. (1983); *Islam is the all Divine Messages in one.* Vol. I; I.P.B. Lagos, Nigeria, p. 180.

[9] Ch 90 v. 4

> It is We who created them and We have made their joints strong.[10]

Because of the endurance and strength given to man so as to bear all the sufferings of hard work in his struggle to achieve success and glory, the end result is a pleasant one as stated in the Holy Qur'an thus:

> Then, he whose balance (of good deeds) will be (found) heavy, will be in a life of good pleasure and satisfaction.[11]

One fact that remains certain, is that anyone who works for his livelihood, keeping in mind the pleasure of God in his work, will be like the mother of Moses (Musa) who receives wages for feeding her own child i.e. one will earn his living as well as reward from God for honestly carrying out his work.

The best and dignified work

Any type of work by which a Muslim can earn a living without doing, supporting or propagating anything harmful (unlawful) is permitted. This will refute the view of some people who regard certain kinds of work (or professions) as contemptible; as the Holy Prophet (SAW) Himself denied the validity of such a notion. He said the whole of human being's dignity is tied up with his work and that what is even a real disgrace and humiliation consist in one depending on other people for help.

He further said:

> It is better that a person should take a rope and bring a bundle of wood on his back to sell so that Allah may preserve his honour, than that he should beg from people (regardless of) whether they give to him or refuse him.[12]

---

[10] Ibid., Ch.76 v. 28.

[11] Ch.101 v. 6-7.

[12] Imam Malik (1982); *Al-Muwatta*, Diwan Press, England, p. 500.

Also, Zubair Ibn Awam related that the Holy Prophet (SAW) said:

> That one of you should take up his cords, go to the mountain, carry a pile of wood on his back, sell it and thereby make his face secure against the chastisement of Allah would be better for him than asking people, whether they give him or not.[13]

Also, Abu Hurairah relates that the Holy Prophet (SAW) said:

> That one of you should carry a pile of wood is better for him than asking from someone whether he gives him or not.[14]

The foregoing shows that the best and most dignified work is the one done with ones hands i.e. through labour.

The Holy Prophet (SAW) said:

> No one has ever earned a living better than by working with his own hand: Dawud (David) the Prophet of Allah earned his living by the work of his own hand.[15]

Also, Abu Hurairah relates that the Holy Prophet (SAW) said:

> David, the Prophet of Allah ate only out of his earnings from his labour.[16]

In another version of the *Hadith*, it is stated that Miqdad Ibn Ma'dikarib relates that the Holy Prophet (SAW) said:

> No one has eaten better food than that procurred through the labour of his hands. David, the Prophet of Allah ate only out of his earnings from his

---

[13] Khan, M. Z. (1985); *Riyadh as-Salihin*, Vols. 1 and 2 of Imam al-Nawawi (*Garden of the Righteous*); p. 309.

[14] Ibid.

[15] Transmitted by Bukhari; as quoted by Higab M (1983), ibid., p. 179.

[16] Khan, M. Z. (1985), ibid., p. 309.

labour.[17]

This shows that in earning a living, great importance is attached to physical labour - i.e. using ones hands rather than staying idle or begging. It is reported that once an unemployed man of the Ansar (helpers) asked the Holy Prophet (SAW) for some charity. The Holy Prophet enquired from him if he had any property. He replied that he had a blanket to cover his body and a cup to drink with. The Prophet asked him to bring those things. When he brought them, the Holy Prophet (SAW) took them in His hand and auctioned them among the people. One of those present offered one dirham. The Prophet requested him to raise the bid. Another man offered 2 dirhams and bought them. The Holy Prophet (SAW) gave the 2 dirhams to the man and advised him to purchase an axe, and when he did the Holy Prophet fixed the handle in it with his own hands. Giving it to that man he said 'go to the jungle and cut wood and don't come to see me before 15 days.' After a fortnight, when he came back, the Holy Prophet (SAW) enquired how he was. He replied that he earned 12 dirhams during that period and purchased some cloth and grain. The Holy Prophet (SAW) remarked, 'This is better than begging and disgracing yourself on the day of judgement.'[18]

In order to lend credence to labour, it is an established fact that almost all the Prophets had to work for their living. The Holy Prophet (SAW) is a perfect example, because he worked as a hired hand looking after sheep belonging to some citizens in Makkah. He said: 'There is no Prophet, sent by Allah who has not worked as a shepherd.' His companions asked him 'You also, messenger of Allah? He said: 'yes, I have looked after the flocks for citizens of Makkah in return for small payment.'[19]

Also, He (the Prophet) was engaged in wood-cutting. During one of His trips, Holy Prophet (SAW) suggested that a goat be cooked. One of the companions said: 'O Messenger of Allah, I undertake to slaughter it.' Another said: I undertake to skin it. A third said: 'I undertake to cook it'. The Holy Prophet then said: 'I undertake to cut wood for fuel'. The companions said: 'O Messenger of Allah, we can cut the wood instead of you'. The Prophet said: 'I know that you are willing to

---

17 Ibid., p. 310.

18 Transmitted by Tirrmidhi and Abu Dawud; as quoted by Higab M (1983), ibid., p. 180.

19 Higab, M. (1983), ibid., p. 180.

relieve me, but I hate being distinguished over you, because Allah hates seeing a servant of His being distinguished over his companions'. Then the Prophet got up and cut wood.[20]

Other Prophets like Dawud (David) worked as an artisan and blacksmith, Noah as a boat maker, Zul-Qarnian engaged in construction of iron well, Musa (Moses) as a hireling, Zakarriyya (Zakariah) as carpenter. It was related by Abu Hurairah that the Holy Prophet (SAW) said: "Zakariah was a carpenter."[21]

Also, Prophet's companions were also labourers. The morning after Caliph Abu Bakr had been chosen as a Caliph, he carried on his head the cloth he was engaged in selling. He hurried to the market and wanted to resume his work as a trader, but Umar Ibn khattab and some other companions dissuaded him, saying: 'How can you do this when you have been made responsible for the affairs of the Muslims?' Abu Bakr answered: 'How, then, can I feed my dependents'? They said: 'We will establish a salary for you.' And Abu Bakr was given ½ a sheep everyday. Abdul-Rahman ibn Awf refused the offer given by his host, Sa'd ibn al Rabi' al-Ansari by giving him ½ of his possessions and chose to work as a trader in the markets of Madina instead of being supported by him.[22]

There is no labour, as long as it is lawful, that is contemptible, a source of shame or degrading, for if it is so, Holy Prophet (SAW) will not have worked as a shepherd or wood-cutter, etc.

Also, there was an occasion in which the hands of a companion of the Holy Prophet (SAW) became black (dark) by working with a hammer. The Holy Prophet (SAW) on seeing his hands, enquired as to what had happened. He replied that it was because he had worked with a hammer on a very hard ground to earn a living for his family. Hearing this, the Holy Prophet (SAW) kissed his hands (and was pleased to know that he was earning an honest living by hard work).[23]

The importance of labour in Islam has then been summed up by Imam Sarakhsi in these words:

> Search for livelihood (labour) is incumbent upon

---

[20] Ibid.

[21] Khan, M. Z. (1985), ibid., p. 309.

[22] Transmitted by Bukhari: as quoted by Higab, M. (1983), ibid., p. 179.

[23] Nasseef, A.O.; (1982); *Encyclopaedia of Search* Vol. II; The Muslim Schools Trust, London ; p. 516.

> every Muslim.[24]

The classification of work

Based on the above, labour can be classified into physical or manual and intellectual or mental etc. It is regarded as a physical or manual labour when a person uses his skill with the aid of his strength or hands or by rendering services, as what obtained with Prophet Shu'aib, addressing Prophet Musa thus:

> I desire to marry one of my two daughters to thee on condition that thou serve me for eight (8) years; but, if thou complete ten (10), it will be of thy own free will, and I wish not to be hard on thee.[25]

While intellectual or mental labour is such that one is expected to use his skill, knowledge and wisdom to bring about the desired result. This has been referred to in the Holy Qur'an, through a dialogue between Prophet Yusuf and the king of Egypt:

> So the king said: 'Bring him unto me; I will take him especially to serve about my own person. 'Therefore when he had spoken to him, he said: 'Be assured this day, thou art, before our own presence, with rank firmly established, and fidelity fully proved: (Joseph) said: 'Set me over the store-houses of the land: I will indeed guard them, as one that knows (their importance)'. Thus did we give established power to take possession therein as, when, or where he pleased. We bestow of our mercy on whom we please, and we suffer not, to be lost, the reward of those who do good.[26]

The above supports that every effort, manual or intellectual, of man

---

[24] Ibid., p. 505.

[25] Ch.28 v. 27.

[26] Ch. 12 v. 54-56.

is rewarded in the form of increased prosperity and better living.

The supply of labour is done through efficiency which is the ability to work with industry, skill and intelligence to increase productivity of capital.

Efficiency, generally, depends on the following:

i) *Physical and mental health.* This has great bearing on the efficiency of workers. A strong and healthy labour is more efficient than a weak and sickly one; just as an honest and conscientious workers, we realizes his duty and responsibility, will work harder and more diligently than a dishonest person.

ii) *Mental fitness.* Here, intelligence and general ability is another important factor which affects efficiency of labour. An able and intelligent man can do better than a stupid and dull one.

iii) *Education and training.* This also increases efficiency because a trained and educated labourer works more efficiently than an untrained and uneducated one. The output and efficiency of an ignorant and untrained worker can not be equal to that of an educated and trained one.

The *physical* and *manual* work

The best work is that in which one uses his own hands. This is authenticated by the following traditions of the Holy Prophet (SAW):

> No one has ever earned a living better than by working with his own hand: Dawud (David), the Prophet of Allah, earned his living by the work of his own hand.[27]
>
> Ali, the fourth caliph, used to say (with pride) that one day he came to know that the Holy Prophet was hungry. He went in search of work so that he might earn something for the Holy Prophet. He saw a Jew in a garden outside Madinah who had a

[27] Transmitted by Bukhari as quoted by Higab, M. (1983), ibid., p. 179.

> deap of mud and wanted someone to put water into it. He struck a bargain with him at one date for a bucket of water and earned 17 dates in wages for 17 buckets of water and then came home. Then he went to the Holy Prophet and informed him about the bargain and they both ate the dates.[28]

(a) The agricultural work

There are encouragements by the Shari'ah, for man to engage in agricultural activity (including animal husbandry) and as a divine favour it has been made easy. But whatever is to be cultivated has to be *halal* (permitted) and not *haram* (prohibited). And it is not an excuse that one is cultivating that which is *haram* for the sake of non-Muslims.

Its importance has been pointed out to the extent that anyone who engages in agriculture will not only benefit from it in this world, but will get the rewards in the Hereafter resulting from it - i.e. whether the product is eaten or used, sold or even stolen.

The following Quranic verses and Prophetic traditions will testify to that:

> (i) It is He who has spread out the earth for (His) creatures: therein is fruit and date-palms, producing sheathed fruit stalks enclosing date); also corn, with (its) leaves and stalk for fodder and sweet – smelling plants. Then which of the favours of your Lord will ye deny?[29]

> (ii) Then let man look at his food, (and how we provide it): for that we pour forth water in abundance, and we split the earth in fragments, and produce therein corn, and grapes and nutritious plants, and olives and dates, and enclosed gardens, dense with lofty trees, and fruits

---

[28] Khan, M. M. (1976), ibid., p. 202.

[29] Ch.55 v. 10-13.

> and fodder, for use and convenience to your cattle.[30]

The Prophet (SAW) said:

> (iii) When a Muslim plants or cultivates a crop, no bird or human being eats from it without its being accounted as a (rewardable) charity for him.'[31]

He also said:

> (iv) When a Muslim plants a plant, anything eaten of it or stolen from it, until the Day of Resurrection, is accounted as a charity for him.[32]

Once a man passes by a companion of the Prophet, Abu al-Darda while he was planting a walnut tree. The man said, 'Are you planting this even though you are a very old man? This tree will not bear fruit for many years.' 'what of it?' Abu al-Darda replied. 'Others will eat of its fruits, and the reward will be mine.'[33]

(b) The industrial and professional work

With the modern technological and scientific thought, from the Islamic point of view, it would be extremely undesirable if people should limit their economic efforts solely to agriculture. This would expose the Muslims to multi-faceted dangers such as defeat, humiliation, loss of religious freedom, etc. This explains why the Muslims apart from agriculture, must develop areas such as industries, professions, science and technology, etc., which are essential for the life, strength and power, posterity and wealth of a community.

These are not merely permitted and necessary, but regarded as Fard

---

[30] Ch. 80 v. 24-32.

[31] Transmitted by Bukhari and Muslim as quoted by Qaradawi Y. (1984), ibid., p. 129.

[32] Transmitted by Muslim, as quoted by Qaradawi Y. (1984), ibid., p. 129.

[33] Al-Qaradawi, Yusuf (1984); *Al-Halal wal Haram fil Islam (The lawful and the prohibited in Islam)*Translated by K. El-Helbawy; M.M Siddique and Syed Shukry; I.I.F.S.O. (Kuwait), p. 129.

Kifaya- 'the obligations of sufficiency'. Any shortage of qualified persons in these fields (which are regarded as essential) they entire Muslim community is to be blamed, especially those in positions of authority. This has been succinctly explained by Imam al-Ghazzali thus:

> Sciences (technology inclusive) whose knowledge is deemed Fard Kifayah comprise every area which is indispensable for the welfare of this world, such as the following: Medicine, which is necessary for the life of the body; arithmetic, for daily transactions and the division of legacies and inheritances, as well as others besides. These are the sciences without which, because of their absence, a community would be reduced to narrow straits. But should one who can practice them arise in the community, it would suffice, and the obligation to acquire their knowledge would cease to be binding upon the rest of the community. No one should be surprised when we say that medicine as well as arithmetic are of the sciences which are fard kifayah, as are the basic industries such as agriculture, weaving, politics and even cupping and tailoring: for if a town should lack a cupper, extinction would overtake its people, and they would be driven to expose themselves to destruction. Has not He who has sent down the Malady also sent down the remedy, given guidance for its use and prepared the means for administering it? It is not therefore, permissible to expose oneself to destruction by neglecting the remedy.[34]

The industrial and professional work, include iron works, building works, construction of dams, architecture, shepherding, tailoring, weaving, plumbing, carpentry, hunting, mining work, etc., but, those not permitted include prostitution, manufacturing of intoxicants and

---

[34] Faris, N.A.; (1966); *Ihya 'Ulum al-Din*, Vol. I (the Book of Knowledge); sh. Muhammad Ashraf, Lahore , Pakistan, p. 37.

drugs, making of statues, etc.

Looking at the trend today, Muslims are really lagging in the field of science and technology. A good example is in the field of medicine, in which male doctors, physiotherapists and nurses examine female patients, which is highly condemned in Islam. It is time, long over due, we correct this anomaly.

The office work (salaried employment)

Every Muslim is free to seek for employment, be it in the service of the government, corporation, company, an organization or an individual as long as the job is lawful. So that, one cannot seek for employment in say brewing company, as that will be injurious to Muslims and Islam generally. The same goes with organizations i.e. bands dealing in usury (interest), factory which manufactures armaments to be used against Muslim etc. in other words, any office work that brings about more input and benefit to the society is permitted. The Islamic guideline in aspiring for positions in government, company, organization and the like is that one should be *fit* and *competent* for the job.

But the trend nowadays, is that fitness and competency is overridden by *nepotism* and *godfatherism*. Then, let them be warned for Abu Hurairah reported the Prophet (p.b.u.h) saying,

> Woe to the rulers, the leaders, and the trustees. On the Day of Resurrection some people will wish that they could be suspended between heaven and earth rather than having had the burden of their responsibilities.[35]

The best thing is that whoever is not qualified for a job or post should not be given. In this regard, the Holy Prophet (SAW) has set an example. Abu Dharr narrated, 'I said, Messenger of Allah; will you not appoint me?'. The Prophet (p.b.u.h) petted me on the shoulder and then said, Abu Dharr, you are a weak person, and this is a trust; and on the Day of Resurrection it will be a cause of regret and shame except for the one who qualifies for it and fulfils his responsibilities.[36]

---

[35] Transmitted by Bukhari as quoted by Higab, M. (1983), ibid., p. 179.

[36] Transmitted by Muslim as quoted by Qaradawi, Y. (1984), ibid., p. 129.

The intellectual work

In this type of work, one is expected to use his faculty of reasoning (i.e. mind) to a thing coupled with his skill and hard work to bring about a desired result.

The Holy Qur'an referred to intellectual work per the dialogue between the Prophet Yusuf and the king of Egypt:

> ...(Joseph) said: Set me over the storehouses of the land: I will indeed guard them, as one that knows (their importance).[37]

This type of work can best be appreciated in terms of computer technology. We have seen inventions that are highly computerised and eased a lot of work, which if it were to be done manually will require greater input. Also, the manual work which involves hand work can be spurred into greater heights, if intellectualism is added. It is also, applicable to a situation where a person is employed for a particular job; given terms of reference and then left entirely free to use his intellect, skill, knowledge and hard work to bring about the desired result. This is particularly so, in the private sector, in which the management strives to maximise profit.

The qualities of a good worker

There are certain qualities required of a good worker; Viz.

(1) Competency

The first and foremost quality of a good worker is that he must be competent and qualified for the job. If he is not competent he may cause harm, as grave as injustice in the case of judiciary, death in the case of medical treatment, and loss of liberty and independence in the case of ruling. It is also regarded as deception on the part of the Muslim community. Any work that is spoiled by ignorance, inexperience, or

---

[37] Ch. 12 v. 54 -56.

lack of training, will make the unqualified worker not only responsible in this world, but also in the hereafter, as it is indicated by the Holy Prophet (S.A.W.) thus:

> Judges are three: two will be in Hell, and one will be in paradise. The man who knows the truth and gives judgment contrary to it, will be in Hell; the man whose judgment is based upon ignorance, will be in Hell; but the man who knows the truth and gives judgment in accordance with it, will be in paradise.[38]

The worker is expected to do his utmost best to preserve the quality which is necessary for the job. A good example, is the case of a "wet-nurse" who must eat and drink what enriches her milk, since this is necessary for carrying out fully the duty of lactation, as neglecting it is harmful to the child she is nursing."[39]

The employer is free to annul the employment where there is decrease in this quality.

(2) Efficient and strong

Not only must the worker be competent and qualified, he must be efficient and strong. This quality has been noticed and evident in the words of the daughter of Shu'aib in the following Quranic verse thus:

> O my (dear) father: engage him on wages: truly the best of men for thee to employ is the (man) who is strong and trusty.[40]

One makes a good and efficient worker out of himself when he has the strength or ability. But it is not in every work that physical strength is necessary. This varies from work to work. Prophet Yusuf asked to be appointed as a treasurer of Egypt because of his experience and honesty, not because of his physical strength.

---

[38] Ch. 12 v. 54-56.

[39] Ibn Qudamah; (n.d), Mughni vol. VII; pp. 627-629.see al-Barrah, Z.A. (1964); *Ahkam awlad fi-Islam*; Al-Darul Kawmiyyah Publishing Co. (Cairo) pp. 31-35.

[40] Ch.28 v. 26.

(3) Punctuality

Punctuality to work, or the doing of the work in time is important. Umar, the second caliph advised workers to be punctual in their work by his famous saying:

> Do not postpone today's work to the next day lest work over-burden you.[41]

Punctuality to work is an added quality as far as a worker is concerned, showing dedication and efficiency. But, late coming to work is a sign of laziness, inefficiency and this attitude is contemptible. The trend today in Nigeria is that people go to work late and leave early; postpone the day's work to a later day and the end result is nothing but inefficiency and a great loss to the community.

(4) Honesty and trustworthiness

This quality is required of a good worker and it implies justice, truthfulness and faithfulness in judges, lawyers, witnesses, traders, lecturers, treasurers, cashiers, store-keepers, private secretaries, etc. In short, in all kinds of work.

The nature of honesty required in every occupation differs according to the nature of the occupation itself. Prophet Musa (Moses) proved to be an honest man, quite worthy of being trusted with people's honour. This was recognised by the daughter of Prophet Shuaib. He accompanied her to receive her father's reward by watering his sheep, and as the day was stormy, he said to the young lady: 'Do not walk in front of me let the wind reveals your figure; but walk behind me and direct me by saying go right or go left.'[42]

This kind of honesty is necessary in those who have occupations similar to that of Musa, when he served Shu'aib. It is also necessary to domestic servants who usually mix with the employer's family and physicians whose nature of profession necessitates the examination of the woman's body, etc.

---

[41] Transmitted by the Ibn al-Jawzi, as quoted by Higab M. (1983), ibid., p. 180.

[42] Interpretation of the Holy Qur'an, by al-Tabari.

(5) Knowledgeability

The work of an educated and trained worker increases efficiency. To have knowledge in the particular field in which one is employed is equated to abundant wealth and riches. The ignorant and untrained worker cannot be equal to that of an educated and trained one. This is explained in the Holy Qur'an, thus:

> Say: Are those equal, those who know and those who do not know?[43]

This shows intimate relationship between human progress and education. A worker who wants to be knowledgeable so that he can increase efficiency needs training, which can be in the form of courses, in-training services, seminars, symposia, workshops, etc. Otherwise, an ignorant and untrained worker is equated to the man whose judgment is based upon ignorance in the prophet' tradition that among three judges, two are going to hell, among which is the one who judged ignorantly.[44]

(6) Freedom of work

Freedom of work is fully guaranteed in Islamic law. Everyone can do any work he likes and move from one place to another without restrictions in search for work with better wages. This will go a long way in improving the standard of living of the community. A Muslim living and working in area or places with scarce means can move to another area where he can find abundant resources and greater prosperity.

Within a country, disparity exists in terms of wages among the places of work. The tendency is there is always the exodus of workers to where they will get better pay. This is so, not to talk of what obtains from country to country. The only way out is to allow such freedom which is an effective and appropriate method of solving many of the economic and socio-political evils of modern times. It will also facilitate the standardization of wages all over the community in a

---

[43] Ch. 39 v. 9.

[44] Ch. 12 v. 54 – 56.

country, if there are no restrictions on immigration of foreign workers to that country. This conclusion can be deduced from the following Quranic verse thus:

> And God Has made the earth for you as a carpet (spread out), that ye may go about therein, in spacious roads.[45]

The idea of moving around in search of a better work is evident and necessary from the fact that some area are drought stricken, making it barren, and the end result is that people have to migrate to fertile areas. The same goes with non-industrial centres; because industrial centres will witness the mass exodus of workers to the neglect and desertion of non-industrial centres. It tells why certain areas are more populated than others.

Rights and protection of worker

An individual employed to work either for an individual, government, company or organization is definitely placed in a comparatively weaker position and his interest is likely to be jeopardized by the person who employed him (who is in possession of the capital). Hence, the need for protecting him specially and guaranteeing his rights as far as the work is concerned. The protection of the individual worker is uppermost if we view the situation that even working animals like donkey, horse, cow, etc., need protection.

The Holy Prophet (SAW) enjoined all those who had working animals to observe 3 conditions:[46]

(1) They should be taken to work when fresh and relieved of work when still fresh (and not to be overworked); and

(2) Suitable arrangements must be made at proper intervals for feeding, water and rest.

They should not be beaten and sworn at. In short, one is to use them

[45] Ch. 71 v. 19 - 20.

[46] Transmitted by Bukhari as quoted by Higab, M. (1983), ibid., p. 179.

moderately, and that is why the Holy Prophet (SAW) did not hesitate to tell a woman that she deserved Hell merely because she kept a cat tied without food and water.[47]

And the reverse in the case, as narrated by Abu Hurairah that Holy Prophet (S.A.W) said Allah Had forgiven a prostitute because she saved the life of a thirsty dog by giving it water.[48]

If that is the case with animals in guaranteeing and protecting their rights, then an individual worker deserves more than that. Therefore, the following are the rights of the worker:

(1) Wages (salary)

The worker is entitled to a wage (salary) which will enable him to enjoy a decent standard of living. This right is very important, and that is why the Holy Prophet (SAW) forbids the employment of any worker without first settling his wages.[49]

There are many definitions of wages, by Muslim and non-Muslim writers, the best definition is one by Professor Bentham:

> A wage may be defined as a sum of money paid under contract by an employer to a worker for a service rendered.[50]

Among the Muslim writers, the best definition is one in which wages is defined as:

> The price which is paid to the labourer (worker) for his services in the production of wealth.[51]

As long as a worker is fully employed and is carrying out his duty according to the terms of the employment, he is entitled to be paid his

---

[47] Ibid.

[48] Ibid.

[49] Karim F.A. (1939), *Al-Hadis Mishkat-ul-Masabih,* The Book House, Lahore Book II p. 301.

[50] *Economics* (1940) 2nd Edition, p. 231, as quoted by *Naseef, A.O. (1982); Encyclopedia of Seerah vol. II*; The Muslim Schools Trust, London, p. 557.

[51] Ibid.

wages as of right. This is absolutely recognized by the sharia. They Holy Qur'an says:

> And if the suckle (your offspring) give them their due payment.[52]

Just as is the case of wet-nurses referred to in the above Qur'anic verse, every worker has the same right to be paid for his work.

In this connection, the Holy Prophet (SAW) warned against employing workers, getting the work fully performed, but refusing to give them their wages.[53] This right of a worker to have his wages fully paid should be respected at all costs, and it is even better to adopt and to go as far the popular saying of the Holy Prophet (SAW) thus:

> Let him who can, be like the man of the measure of rice.[54]

The exhortation of the Muslims by the Holy Prophet (SAW) with the above saying is based upon a narration in which He made, praising and admiring the gesture of one of the three men unable to get out from the mountain cave. The three men once got a shelter in a mountain cave when they were attacked by rain. They were unable to get out of the cave because of rock that rolled down from the mountain until it covered the mouth of the cave. Then they said to each other 'think about a good deed you have done for the sake of Allah, then ask Allah by its merit, to move away the rock and uncover the cave.' They asked Allah, every one by the merit of the deed done, until the rock was completely moved, and the cave was uncovered. They got out safely. The merit of the deed of the third man is the one relevant to our theme (wage). He said: 'once, I hired a man for a measure of rice,' when he finished his work, he said to me: 'give me my wage.' When I offered it to him, he refused. I sowed the rice that the labourer deserved as a wage until I collected from the profits of investing it, cows and their shepherds. Then he came and said: 'Have fear of Allah and give me my wage.' I then said: Have fear of Allah and do not ridicule me', I answered: 'I am not ridiculing you, so take the cows and their

---

[52] Ch.56 v. 6.

[53] Higab, M; (1983), ibid., p. 179.

[54] Ibid., p. 195.

shepherds', and the man took them.'[55]

What is happening today is in contrast to the story above. Workers are employed but when the work is fully performed, they are either not paid exactly as agreed upon or not paid at all.

There are many factors that must be borne in mind in determining wages as to its minimum or maximum. Some of them are the ability (physical or mental) of the worker, nature of his work and his economic responsibilities, length of service of a person, time and money spent acquiring necessary knowledge, skill and training for a trade, the extent of actual economic needs, number of dependants (an addition of a child to the family of a government servant should mean an increase in his allowance from the treasury), change in the responsibility of a job, and above all through negotiation between workers, employer and the state.

In short, wages are determined in a most equitable fashion without undue favour to, or undue oppression on, any side. Each party gets its legitimate share of the joint product without being unjust to the other;

> Deal not unjustly, and ye shall not be dealt with unjustly.[56]

The differences in wages can exist and can be allowed but not to such an extent as to create wide gap between the low-grade and high-grade workers so as to cause any economic or social friction between the two groups. It should be fixed so that the low-grade can meet all his basic requirements, while the high-grade should not indulge in extravagance or luxuries.

The system which permits unjust differences in salaries of government employees, is very unfair to the low-grade, because it cannot maintain them, let alone to talk of their families on a decent standard of living. This encourages bribery and corruption, and misappropriation of public fund, because of the enforced poverty which weakened the moral character of the people.

To avert all these, there is the need to change the entire wage structure by considering the following:

(i) The minimum wage should be high enough to meet the essential requirements of the worker, bearing in mind the ability of the

---

[55] Ibid.

[56] Ch. 2 v. 279.

employer to pay.

(ii) The economic responsibilities of the worker including the size of his family.

(iii) The difference between the wages should be confined within narrow limit as justified by the natural differences in the nature of work, length of service, education, training and economic needs of such worker.[57]

The wages should not go beyond the limit of these factors. Therefore, in order to maintain wages at a reasonable standard, Islam has given complete freedom of work - i.e. to move about from one place to another or to select any work of one's choice.

(2) He should not be overburdened

The worker should not be given any work which is beyond his strength i.e. physical and mental. If he is entrusted with a work more than he can do, he has to be assisted.

In the Holy Qur'an, it is stated:

> On no soul doth God place a burden greater than it can bear.[58]

The Holy Prophet said:

> Do not impose upon the labourers a job which overcomes them, if you give them a job which is too much for them, you must help them.[59]

(3) He should not be overworked

The worker has the right not to be overworked. This is so, when we take into consideration that the worker has several other duties which

---

[57] Naseef, A.O. (1982), ibid., p. 565.

[58] Ch. 2 v. 286

[59] Transmitted by Muwatta, as quoted by Higab M. (1983), ibid., p.193.

he as a Muslim must perform, such as worshipping Allah, looking after his family, attending to visitors and relations, acquiring religious and mundane knowledge and above all to give his body its rightful rest.

There should be sufficient periods of rest and recuperation, so that he may resume his work efficiently and willingly. So, whatever number of hours will be fixed for a daily work must be done in such a way as to leave for the worker such time needed for carrying out such other several duties. Sufficient rest for a worker is important for efficiency and increased productivity, just as, even in devotional acts, one is not expected to overwork himself as is evident from a tradition of the Holy Prophet narrated by Abdullah ibn Amr that:

> The prophet once came to me and said: 'Have I not been informed, Abdullah, that you keep vigil all night long for worshipping Allah and fast all day long'? I answered: yes, I do.' The Prophet said: 'Do not do so'. Keep awake only for sometime and then sleep, and fast (your voluntary fasting) for a day or some days then break your fast.[60]

(4) The employer should be generous to his employee (worker)

Generosity include showing of kindness, annual increase in wage, free medical treatment, fixing gratuity, gifts to the worker and his family in cash or kind etc. It also includes tolerance and forgiveness, even to the extreme limits of patience. That is why the Holy Prophet (SAW) said:

> We are supposed to forgive them seventy times everyday.[61]

This tradition, even though it relates to domestic servants, it can be inferred that such is the case of a worker, be it in government, company, etc.

---

[60] Ibid.

[61] Ibid., p.195.

Unemployment

When a person is not engaged in any employment as a worker, he is deemed unemployed. The issue of unemployment is one among the numerous problems of the society. It is therefore, the responsibility of the Ummah or the Islamic state to find solution to such a problem by helping the unemployed to earn his living. Where one is unemployed as a result of sickness or being invalid, for one reason or the other, it is incumbent upon the Islamic state (and the employer where the sickness or being invalid was when such an employee was under his employment) to contribute towards providing his basic daily requirements. This is clearly referred to in these words:

> ...we provide for them and for you.[62]

As long as the Islamic state cannot guarantee the basic requirements of the unemployed, the sick or the invalid, will have no right to claim obedience to its laws from its members. The unemployment benefit can be from the *zakat* fund and what is contributed by the employers, so as to maintain the standard of living of the unemployed. In short, unemployment which is more of an economic and social problem can best be solved with the internal resources of a country - i.e. *zakat* fund, taxes, etc. - without resorting to foreign aid, contrary to what is obtainable today. This will help in asserting the economic and political independence of the country concerned. With the *zakat* funds, the contributions by the employers and the like, the problem of unemployment can be solved and that is why during Caliph Umar's time, there were excesses of *zakat*, and nobody cared for it.

---

[62] Ch.17 v. 31.

Chapter 3

Sale

The most frequent mode of acquisition and transfer of (private) ownership is effected by sale. The acquisition and transfer of private ownership through this means devolves by the freewill and choice of the party or parties concerned.

Sale has been variously defined. In its ordinary sense it means a transfer of property in turn for money.[1] This definition includes barter and loan transactions.

The definition of sale as a transfer of property for property is restrictive in the sense that anything that does not answer the description of property cannot be the subject-matter of sale, as in the case of mere or proprietary rights, because they cannot be sold.

But the Hannafi School is of the view that proprietary rights can be property, hence can be sold out as it is connected with a lasting specific property. Therefore the better definition which seems to be a comprehensive one is that, sale is the transfer of property or proprietary rights in return for money.[2]

In a sale transaction, there is alienation of property for exchange of money, or exchange of property for property with mutual consent of both parties.

The nature of how human beings are created is such as to be dependent upon one another and impracticable to own all that one needs. Hence, the need for a sale transaction; as a person may have something which others do not have and which he can spare; and at the

---

1 Rahim. A; (1978); *The Principles of Muhammadan Jurisprudence*: All Pakistan Legal Decisions, Lahore, p. 290.

2 Ibid.

same time may need something which others have and which they can spare. The exchange through buying and selling becomes inevitable as it makes the social and economic life function smoothly and encourages people to be productive and to engage in trade and commercial transactions.

This is evident from the example of the Holy Prophet (SAW) and that of His companions. The Holy Prophet established a market place of Banu Qaynuqa which had the most trading activity. Among the companions of the Holy Prophet (SAW) we find skilled traders, craftsmen, farmers and every other kind of professionals and workers.[3]

Abu Bakr al-Siddiq (the first Caliph) was a perfect example, who even on the day on which he was elected caliph hurried to the market to resume his work as a trader. But he was discouraged by people like Umar Ibn Khattab and other companions by establishing a salary for him.[4] It was reported that he was given half a sheep everyday. Many other companions from both the *muhajirun* (emigrants) and the *ansar* (helpers) like Umar, Uthman, Abdur Rahman ibn 'Awf; Sa'd ibn al-Rabi, etc., were also engaged in business transactions.[5]

All these, go to show the importance attached to sale as it is evidenced in the Holy Qur'an by referring to it as 'seeking the bounty of Allah' and equating it with those who fight for His cause:

> Others travel through the land, seeking of Allah's bounty. Yet others were fighting in Allah's cause.[6]

Even, when one engages in sale transaction, he should not allow it to distract his attention from his obligation to His Creator:

> The men whom neither business nor sale can divert from the remembrance of Allah nor from regular salat or from giving zakat.[7]

---

[3] Al-Qaradawi, Y. (1984): *The lawful and the prohibited in Islam*; I.I.F.S.O., pp. 140-141

[4] Higab M. (1983); *Islam is the all-Divine Messages in one*. Vol. I; I.P.B. Lagos, pp. 178-179.

[5] Ibid.

[6] Holy Qur'an, Ch.73 v. 20.

[7] Ch. 24 v. 37.

Types of sale

There are four types of sale having regard to the nature of the subject-matter, namely:[8]

(i) *Bai'a* or sale - that is when a determinate article is sold for a price.

(ii) *Muqa'ida* or Barter – a situation when a determinate article is sold for another determinate article.

(iii) *Sarf* or specie of price, that is sale of price from price; and

(iv) *Salam* or sale in advance - the price for certain goods to be delivered in the future on a fixed date.

Among the four types of sale above, the first (*Bai'a* - sale) is the one frequently used. The second, type outlived its usefulness; as a medium of exchange i.e. currency replaced exchange of an article for article. The third type of sale (*sarf*) is effected by mutual delivery of the articles, which among other thing must be in weight. For example, when gold is sold for silver or vice versa, there must be delivering or both articles at the time of the sale. The fourth type of sale - i.e. *salam* or sale in advance is now been frequented used in our localities. The practices is that crops and fruits, etc., are sold before they are ripe. This type of sale is prohibited. *Salam* only allowed when the goods are to be delivered within a specified period at a fixed price, as the following tradition of the Prophet will show. It was narrated by Ibn Umar that the Prophet said:

> There is no harm in buying foodstuff to be delivered within a specified period at a fixed price provided that it is not standing crops that have not yet become ripe and free from blights and diseases. [9]

---

[8] Rahim A (1978), ibid., p. 290.

[9] Imam Malik (1982), *Al-Muwatta*, Diwan Press, England, p. 294.

Conditions of valid sale

Once a valid sale transaction has been concluded, it has the effect of passing the property in the thing sold to the buyer and the seller to be entitled to the price. This is subject to the following conditions; namely:

i) The subject-matter of the sale transaction must be generally in existence, with the exception of a *salam* sale.

ii) The subject-matter must be lawful, as transacting in things that are unlawful is prohibited.

The Holy Prophet (SAW) said:

> Surely, Allah and His Messenger have prohibited the sale of wine, the flesh or dead animals, swine and idols. [10]

This shows that anything prohibited in general that tends to promote and propagate it among the people thereby encouraging them to do what is unlawful is prohibited.

iii) The subject-matter must be capable of being delivered or possessed.

iv) The subject-matter must be known and certain. Any sale transaction involving uncertainty is to be avoided. In a situation where the uncertainty is of a small magnitude, the sale is not prohibited. It is only prohibited where there is an obvious element of uncertainty which may lead to a dispute and conflict, or may result in the unjust appropriation of other people's money.

v) There must be a valid offer and acceptance. It is only with mutual consent or with a proposal and an acceptance that the sale of a thing is completed.

The Holy Prophet (SAW) is reported to have said:

---

[10] Siddiqi, A.H. (1976), *Sahih Muslim*; Vol. III; Sh. Muhammad Ashraf, Lahore (Pakistan), p. 830.

> The two must not part except by mutual consent. [11]

vi) There must be no deception or fraud on the part of the parties especially the seller. The Holy Prophet (SAW) said:

> When a sale is held, say-there is no cheating. [12]

In another report, Ibn Umar reported the Holy Prophet (SAW) as saying, when a man told the Prophet that he was being deceived, thus:

> When you make a bargain, say, 'there is no attempt to deceive'. [13]

Then, the man-made a habit of saying that:

vii) The parties are allowed to include options in the sale. These options are either to accept or withdraw the offer. Normally, three days' option is allowed for the buyer and seller.
Ibn 'Umar reported the Holy Prophet (SAW) as saying:

> Both parties in a sale transaction have a right to annul it only so long as they have not separated, except in transactions which have been made subject to the right of the parties to annul them. [14]

viii) There should be no price control for property which is the subject-matter of a sale, it should be left to be determined by the market forces of supply and demand. It was reported on the good authority of Abu Huraira that when the Prophet was asked to fix prices, He replied thus:

> Allah is the one who fixes prices, who withholds, who gives lavishly, and who provides. I very much hope to meet Him with no one to claim me for any injustices

---

[11] Karim F.A. (1939), *Mishkat-ul-Masabih,* The Book House, Lahore, Book II, p. 270.

[12] Ibid.

[13] Siddiqi, A.H. (1976), ibid., p. 805.

[14] Ibid.

> with regard to blood or property.[15]

This is not the case where artificial forces, such as hoarding, interfere in the free market. Public interest will take precedence over the freedom of the individual(s) concerned.

(ix) In a sale transaction involving weights and measures, there should be no withholding of the full measure or weight. The Holy Qur'an in this connection says:

> Give full measure when you measure, and weigh with a balance that is straight: That is the most fitting and the most advantageous in the final determination.[16]

And in another verse, the Holy Qur'an is saying:

> Give full measures, and do not be of those who give less (then what is due). And weigh with the straight balance, and do not diminish people's goods nor do evil on the earth, making mischief.[17]

x) Where in a sale, it involves the payment in advance for the purchase of a thing, the thing must be sold to another before it actually comes into the buyer's possession. The Holy Prophet (SAW) said:

> Whoever advances a thing for something, let him not transfer it to others before it comes into his possession.[18]

(xi) There should be no excessive or much swearing while conducting a sale transaction. It was reported that the Holy Prophet said:

> Avoid much swearing while transacting business, for it produces a ready sale, but blots out the blessing.[19]

---

15 Ibn Taymia (1982); *Public Duties in Islam: The Institution of the Hisba*, The Islamic Function, pp. 47-50.

16 Ch.17 v. 35.

17 Ch.26 v. 181-183.

18 Siddiqi A.H. (1976), ibid., p. 801.

19 Karim F.A. (1939), ibid., p. 168.

According to Abu Dhar, the Prophet of Allah said:

> There are three to whom Allah will not speak on the Day of Resurrection, whom He will not purify, and they will have a painful punishment. They are the losers and disappointed...Who are they, Messenger of Allah? He replied that one of them would be he who produces a ready sale of a commodity by false swearing.[20]

The reason why frequent swearing is to be avoided is two-fold. One, it deceives people and secondly it reduces respect for the name of Allah. By frequent swearing in a sale, one finds markets, but reduces blessing and abundance. Therefore, the Prophet Has warned thus:

> Be careful of excessive oaths in a sale though it finds market, it reduces abundance. [21]

(xii) Parties to a sale transaction are specifically advised by the Holy Qur'an to put it down in writing, especially when the payment or the delivery of the goods or commodity is differed. If on the spot transaction is made hand to hand, there is no need to record them:

> Disdain not to reduce to writing (your contract) for a future period, whether it be small or big: it is more just in the sight of God, more suitable as evidence to and more convenient to prevent doubts among yourselves. But if it be a transaction which you carry out on the spot among yourselves, there is no blame on you if you reduce it not to writing.[22]

(xiii) Parties to a sale or expected to fulfil their legal obligations, especially when they are made merely on trust.[23]

---

[20] Ibid.

[21] Ibid.

[22] Ch. 2 v.282.

[23] Ibid.

Conduct of the parties in a sale transaction

The party (buyer or seller) to a sale transaction is expected to conduct himself in a fair, gentle and kind manner. This is highly expected of him, so as to be showered of the mercy of Allah. Jabir reported Allah's Messenger as saying:

> Allah's mercy is to a man who is kindly when he sells, when he buys and when he makes a claim.[24]

This, again, has been reflected in another tradition thus:

> Before your time, there was a man to whom the Angel came to take his soul and he was asked whether he had done anything good. On his replying that he did not know, he was told to consider, and then he said that the only thing he knew was that he used to have business dealings with people in the world and would demand his rights from them, giving the rich time to pay and letting the poor off.[25]

This was accepted and Allah's mercy showered on him. But the capitalistic tendencies today, do not allow one to be to be fair, gentle and kind in his conduct.

The lawful and unlawful sale transactions

The distinction should be drawn from sale transactions that are lawful and those that are unlawful. This is important for the sake of acquiring the ownership, of property in the lawful way, by the process of selling and buying.

A sale is said to be lawful, where the following conditions are present:

---

[24] Karim, F.A. (1939), ibid., pp. 267-268.

[25] Saddiqi, A.H. (1976), ibid., p. 830.

(i) Legal capacity of the parties

The party to the sale may be one, two or more. Usually, it takes two to make a complete sale. The party/parties must have the legal capacity to conclude a sale i.e. must be adult, sane, free from interdiction, and must be voluntarily undertaking. Absence of these qualities means the party/parties have defective capacity. Also, the parties must have the intention to conclude the sale. That is why intention must be properly expressed.

(ii) The subject matter of the sale

The subject-matter of the sale may be a corpus (the material thing such as land, houses, cars etc.), or usufruct (income, profit or use of a property) or claims (loans, debts, etc.). Also, the subject-matter must be lawful or legally permissible. So, things like pig, wine etc. cannot be the subject matter of a sale. Once all these have been conformed to, and if ownership is acquired through this means, such is deemed lawful.

On the other hand, all unlawful means of acquiring ownership of property, are denounced as it is aptly stated in the Holy Qur'an in the following words:

> And do not eat up your property among yourselves for vanities, nor use it as bait for the judges, with intent that ye may eat up wrongfully and knowingly a little of (other) people's property.[26]

This shows, robbery, theft, misappropriation, bribery, gambling, usury etc. are prohibited as being false or dishonest means of acquiring property. The reason, being that it promotes the habits of indolence, a negation of honest labour, and reduces some members of the society to penury while others prosper at their expense.

---

[26] Ch. 2 v. 188.

Chapter 4

Hiba [gift]

The word 'gift' (*hiba*) has been variously defined by the Muslim scholars. One of the functional definitions of it is thus:

> The immediate and unqualified transfer of the corpus of the property without any return or exchange value by one person to the other, during the lifetime of the donor.[1]

From this definition, it is understood that there should be no condition or restrictions attached to it, otherwise, a gift, will be unenforceable. The intention of the donor must be demonstrated by his entire relinquishment of the thing given.

Also, from the above definition, it is understood that any free grant of ownership made from a pious or religious motive, is not considered as an ordinary gift (*hiba*) but is *sadaqah*.[2]

Every Muslim, male, or female, who has attained maturity and is of sound mind, may make a gift. The Holy Prophet (SAW) encouraged exchange of gifts between people to increase love between them. This is evidenced from the following traditions of the Holy Prophet (SAW):

(i) "Give presents (and gifts) to one another, for a present removes grudges."[3] In another narration, it was stated thus:

---

[1] Fyzee, A.A.: (1974): *Outlines of Muhammadan Law*: p. 365.

[2] Tyabji, F.B. : (1919): *Principles of Muhammadan Law*: p. 365.

[3] Fyzee, A.A.: (1974): *Outlines of Muhammadan Law*: p. 365.

(ii) "Give present to one another, for a present removes hatred from the breast..."[4]

Also, in another tradition it says,

(iii) "Exchange gifts among yourselves and thus strengthen mutual love, with each other."[5]

Based on these prophetic traditions, the Holy Prophet asked people, not to reject gifts and also to thank givers which can be done by commendation.

Gift distinguished from other related concepts

There are certain concepts which bear some similarity with gift, and unless distinguished may likely be confused with it. These related concepts to be distinguished here are *sadaqah* (alms deed) and *ariya.*

Gift distinguished from *sadaqah* (alms, deed)

Saduqah can be viewed either in the widest or in the strictest. In the widest, *sadaqah* is any pious or charitable act - i.e. a smile in the neighbour's face or to help the weary, etc. But in the strictest sense, *sadaqah* is the gratuitous act of giving a gift with the object of obtaining merit in the eyes or sight of God. The distinction between gift and *sadaqah* lies in the fact that the motive of gift is *secular*, while the motive of *sadaqah* is *religious*. Also, *sadaqah* is irrevocable once it is made. This is not the case with a gift, as it can be revoked.[6]

Gift distinguished from *ariya*

Ariya is the transferring of the right to enjoy the use or profits of a property without any return. In this type of gift, the period of which it is

---

[4] Ibid.

[5] Ibid.

[6] Hamilton Charles (1979): *The Hedaya – Commentary on the Islamic Laws*: Kitab Bhavan New Delhi; p. 489

made may or may not be specified and revocable at will. The chief distinguishing factor here, is that, in gift, the transferee acquires the right to the property itself, whilst in *ariya* he only obtains the use or beneficial enjoyment for a limited time and the property does not pass to him. In *ariya*, the use may relate to a future time, revocable at will of the donor and acceptance is not a condition. This is not the case in a gift.[7]

Conditions for a valid gift

For a gift to be complete and valid there are certain conditions to be complied with,[8] namely:

i) There must be an offer or proposal or declaration or a manifestation of the wish to give on the part or the donor (*al-wahib*), which must be expressed in clear and unequivocal words for the transfer of property by means of gift, such as 'I have given you'. From this, it should clearly appear that the donor intends to transfer his property by way of gift and to divest himself of all ownership and dominion over the property. Otherwise, the gift is null and void.

   A gift may be made either orally or in writing; but in order to have proper evidence of the transaction, the gift in writing is to be preferred.

ii) There must be an acceptance by the donee (*al-Mawhub lahu*) or his agent either expressly or impliedly of, the declaration of the transfer of property made by the donor, by means of gift. It must be established that the gift was accepted by the donee.

iii) There must be the delivery of the possession of the subject-matter of gift, which is either actually or constructively.

For example, where the subject-matter of the gift is a house, and the donor vacates possession in pursuance of the gift and the donee occupies it, there is an actual possession of the property, the subject matter of the gift. But, where the key to the house is given to the donee,

---

[7] Ibid.

[8] Hussain Imtiyaz (1989): *Muslim Law and Customs*; Kashmir – Srinagar Law Journal Publication, p. 302.

who is turn entrusted it to an agent, delivery of possession is deemed to be constructive. When this happens, there is a valid and completed gift.

In a situation, where a gift is effected, and possession has not been taken of the subject-matter by the donee, but remains entirely at the disposal of the donor and on his death it will descend to his heirs and not to the done.[9]

The best thing to do in the case of delivery of possession is to have documentary evidence showing that delivery has been effected.

There are certain exceptions[10] regarding delivery of possession:

a) Where the donee is already in possession of the subject-matter of the gift;

b) Where the donor or someone holds the property as a trustee or agent of the donee;

c) Where the donor and the donee are both residing at the time of gift as an overt act by the donor indicating a clear indication on his part to transfer possession and to divest himself of all control over the subject of the gift is enough;

d) Where the property is in the possession of some other person;

e) Where the nature of the property does not admit of physical delivery;

f) Where the donee is the husband or wife of the donor; and

g) Where the father or mother makes a gift to a son or daughter.

In all these cases, whether movable or immovable property, physical possession is not a must to complete the gift.

Structure of a gift

(1) Sighah (Formation)

There must be an offer and acceptance. Acceptance is necessary and can be by words or conduct (action).

---

[9] Rahim A; (1978); *The Principles of Muhammadan Jurisprudence*; All Pakistan Legal Decisions, Lahore ; p. 289.

[10] Higab M; (1983); *Islam is the all-Divine Messages in one*. Vol. I; I.P.B, Lagos , p. 223

The Maliki, Shafi'i and Hambali schools are of the view that a gift transaction is bilateral in nature - i.e. involving two parties, one to make the offer and the other to accept it. It shows that acceptance is necessary.[11]

But according to Hannafi school, the gift transaction is unilateral in nature offer is sufficient to the declaration of the gift. To this school, acceptance is not a must to validate a gift; and what matters is delivery of the subject matter; that is a must.[12]

But Shafi'i school differ with Maliki and Hanbali school and supported Hanafi school that the delivery of possession is a must.[13]

(2) Al-Wahib [Donor]

The donor (*al-wahib*) is the one who is making the declaration or offer to transfer the ownership of a property to another person. For him to have such a capacity, he must be:[14]

i) an adult;

ii) sane person;

iii) the lawful owner of the subject matter;

iv) entering such a contract voluntarily - i.e., there should be no force or duress, otherwise it will be invalid.

The problem that may arise, is in relation to a donor who is in a state of *mard-ul-Maut* (death sickness), effecting a gift. Its validity depends on:[15]

i) it should not exceed ⅓ of the property;

ii) it should not be in favour of an heir.

---

[11] Ibid.

[12] Ibid.

[13] Ibid.

[14] Ibid.

[15] Ibid.

(3) Al-Mawhub Lahu [Donee]

The donee (*al-Mawhub lahu*) is the one who is accepting the declaration or offer by the donor to transfer the ownership of a property to him. Whoever is a donee to a gift must have the capacity to receive the gift. This includes minor and insane person under a guardian. The donee must be *actually living* at the time of the gift. Therefore, gift to an unborn child or person not yet in existence is void. The donee can also be an object such as mosque building, school or charitable institution. The donee can even be a non-Muslim, etc.[16]

Donation subject-matter (*Al-mawhub*)

The subject-matter of whatever may be given out as a gift must be:

(i) Legal subject-matter of contract. It is reported that a man brought a cask of wine to the Holy Prophet (S.A.W.) as a gift. The Holy Prophet (S.A.W.) informed him that Allah Had prohibited it. The man asked the Prophet 'shall I not give it to a Jew as a gift?' The Prophet said 'The one who Has prohibited it Has also prohibited that it be given as a gift to the Jew; [17]

ii) Actually in existence;

iii) valuable;

iv) alienable;

v) transferable; and

vi) certain.

On the issue of 'certain', the schools differ. Hannafi school insists that the subject matter of a gift must be certain or specified. But Maliki school insist that certainty is not a condition, as uncertain subject-matter can be given as a gift like a lost animal or a pregnant animal in

[16] Rahim A, (1978), ibid., p. 301.

[17] Al-Qaradawi, Y; (1984): *The Lawful and the prohibited in Islam;* I.I.F.S.O., p. 73.

which the offspring is given as a gift. Also, it is in this connection that to the Hannafis joint or undivided property (*musha'a*) cannot be the subject-matter of gift. Gift of a thing capable of division is not valid unless the said part is divided off and separated from the property of the donor. But gift of part of an indivisible thing is valid.[18]

The Maliki and Shafi'i schools regarded the donation from a joint property as valid. But Hannafi school did not allow such a donation and where that has been done, it is invalid.[19]

The question as to whether a person can make a gift of the whole of his property has been answered by all the Sunni schools that a man has a right to make the gift of the whole of his property as a gift to a stranger.[20]

When it is a woman, she cannot gift away the whole of her property. The consent of her husband is required and not to gift away more than one-third of her property.[21]

Revocation of a gift

The right to revoke a gift is called *raja'at.* The revocation of a gift is highly condemned by the Holy Prophet (S.A.W.). He said:

> He who retracts a gift is like the dog that devours its vomit.[22]

This tradition emphasizes the importance of gift, and once made should not be withdrawn.

But in another tradition it is stated that:

> No one may take back a gift except a father.[23]

Despite, the above tradition condemning revocation of a gift, one

---

[18] Rahim A, (1978), ibid., p. 298.

[19] Ibid.

[20] Ibn Rushd (n.d.), *Bidayat – al- Mujtahid,* Darul Fikr , Lebanon ; Vol. 2, p. 245.

[21] Ibid.

[22] Khan, M.Z. (1985): *Riyadh as-Salihin of Imam Nawawi* (Garden of the Righteous) Curzon Press, London; p. 744.

[23] Karim, F.A. (1939), ibid., Book II, p. 318.

can still revoke a gift if the need arises.

But in the following circumstances a bar has been placed on revocation of a gift, namely:[24]

a) Where there is the incorporation of an increase with the gift, because in that instance a revocation cannot take place so as to include the increase, since that was not included in the gift.

b) Where the death of one of the parties results. For example, if the donee should die his property shifts to his heir and becomes the same as if it had shifted during his life-time. And if the donor should die his heirs are strangers with respect to the contract; since they made not tender of the thing given.

The issue of whether a donor can revoke a gift is subject to juristic, interpretations. Hannafi school is of the opinion that revocation is allowed before possession by the donee but not afterwards.[25] But the others three Sunni schools, namely Maliki, Shafi'i and Hambali, allowed the revocation of a gift in one case *even after* possession, that is between father and son only, as grandfather or other relatives are not allowed to revoke a gift.

This view of the three schools is in consonance with a prophetic tradition thus:

> No one may take back a gift except a father.[26]

Despite this tradition, the father can do that if it is in the same condition as it was given, otherwise, the father cannot revoke it, especially where the gift is used as a loan or converted into another object.[27]

The revocation must be in express and explicit terms, or by consent of the parties. But in another version, the confirmation of the court or judge is necessary so as to remove any doubt.[28]

---

[24] Hamilton Charles, (1979), ibid., p. 486.
[25] Ibid.
[26] Ibid.
[27] Ibid.
[28] Rahim A, (1978), ibid., p. 302.

Revocation cannot take place in the following circumstances:[29]

i) If either the donor or donee has died.

ii) If the gift is to a charity or Sadaqah

iii) When the thing given has perished in the hands of the donee.

iv) Where it is made to the husband or the wife during the subsistence of marital relationship.

v) Where the subject of the gift cannot be restored in its original form.

vi) If the subject-matter of the gift is a land and the donee erects a building or plants a tree on it, or the property has been improved that the increase cannot be separated - e.g. when a wheat is turned into flour.

---

[29] Ibid. See also B.R. Verma (1980), *Mohammedan Law*, Delhi Law House, 6th ed. p. 492.

Chapter 5

Testate succession

This is another means of acquiring or transferring private ownership. An owner of property is allowed to bequeath one-third of his property for a charitable objective or to anyone excepting a legal heir.

The legal basis for making a will can be traced from the Holy Qur'an and *Sunnah* of the Holy Prophet Muhammad (S.A.W.).

> It is prescribed, when death approaches any of you, if he leave any goods, that he make a bequest to parents and next of kin, according to reasonable usage, this is due from the God-fearing.[1]

In another verse, it is stated thus:

> Those of you who die and leave widows should bequeath for their widows a year's maintenance and residence.[2]

These two verses above are generally known as the "verses of bequests."

The validity of a will in favour of parents and widows, as in the above two verses should not be misunderstood, because the rules in it have been partially abrogated by the famous verses dealing with

---

[1] The Holy Qur'an, Ch. 2 v. 180.

[2] Ch. 2 v. 240

inheritance.[3]

The reason for the partial abrogation is not far-fetched: Almighty Allah Has given opportunity to Muslims of making will and enjoined them to maintain justice in that respect. When this opportunity has been abused, the Holy Qur'an fixed shares for parents, widows and some other near relatives.[4]

The Quranic verses above will be better understood, if we look at the recommendation of bequest as applicable to non-Muslim parents, widows and relatives who are neither Quranic shares nor have the right to inherit.

As to its legal basis in the *Sunnah* of the Holy Prophet (S.A.W.), it was reported by the Prophet's companion, Sa'ad b. Abi Wiqqas:

> The Prophet came to visit me in the year of the farewell pilgrimage. When I was afflicted with a severe illness. I said to him 'O Prophet, you see how ill I am. I have property and no heir except my daughter. Shall I then give away ⅔ of my property as alms?' He replied, 'No'. I said 'A half then? He still said 'No'. I then asked 'a third?' He replied: "A third: And a third is much. It is better than you leave your heirs rich than you should leave them destitute begging from their neighbours.[5]

In another report by another companion of the Prophet by name Sa'd b. Malik, he said: when I was very sick the Prophet visited me and asked:, "Have you made a will?" I replied, "Yes: I have bequeathed all my property to the poor and for pious purposes." The Prophet then advised me: "Bequeath only a one-tenth part of it." I replied, "But my estate is vast and my heirs are rich..." Eventually, the Prophet said: "Then bequest a one-third. A one-third is much.[6]

Because of the importance attached to bequest, the Holy Prophet is reported to have said:

> It is not right for a Muslim who has property to

---

[3] Ch. 4 v. 11, 12 and 176 (They are regarded as 3 fundamental verses on inheritance).

[4] Ibid.

[5] Ibn Qudamah; (n.d.), *al-Mughni*, Lebanon , vol. 6, pp. 1-4

[6] Ibid.

> bequeath, that he should pass two nights without having a written will with him.[7]

From this tradition, it should be understood that the duty or right to make a will is subject to two *limitations*:

(i) Not more than one-third of the property can be disposed of by will.

(ii) No will can be made in favour of an heir; unless others consent to it.

The limitations were placed because it was felt after the Holy Qur'an laid down specific rules for the distribution of inheritance, it was undesirable to allow one to temper with the course of devolution of property through unrestricted rights of making wills.

Definition

By testate succession, it means bequest or will and has been variously defined thus:

(i) "the legal declaration of the intentions of a Muslim with respect to his property, which he desires to be carried into effect after his death."[8]

(ii) "as an assignment of property to take effect after one's death."[9]

Also, as
(iii) "an endowment with property of anything after death."[10]

A will has the legal efficacy only when it is accepted after the testator's death, except when it is dedicated to a pious or charitable purpose that acceptance is not necessary. This is the view of all the schools, excepting Shi'a school which is of the view that the will is

---

[7] Karim, F. A. (1939), *Al-Hadis Mishkat-ul-Masabih;* Book 2, The Book House (Lahore) p. 323.

[8] Tyabji's (n.d.), *Muslim Law*, 4th ed., p. 754

[9] Gurin, A.M.; (1987); *An Introduction to Islamic Law of Succession; (Testate/Intestate)*; (unpublished); C.I.L.S., Ahmadu Bello University ; Zaria .

[10] Hamilton; C. (1963); *The Hedaya- Commentary on the Islamic laws;* Lahore ed.; p. 670.

valid and binding if accepted during the testator's life-time. And refusal to accept during his lifetime may be withdrawn and replaced by the legatee's acceptance after the testator's death.[11]

There is no prescribed form of acceptance as any words or actions indicative of consent suffice. All the schools except Hannafi school agree to that, while Hannafis said acceptance can also be implied.[12]

The acceptance or rejection of a will is irrevocable after the testator's death. The Maliki school said, subsequent acceptance following prior refusal and vice versa, is effective if the testator's legal heirs consent thereto but not to revive one which has lapsed or revoked a will accepted.[13]

Types of will

A will can be classified as follows:

(1) General and specific will

A general will is one in which the gift of property is not so specifically distinguished, because it may be a pecuniary legacy or a gift of property generally described. Also, it consists of a share in the entirety of the testator's property or a share in a particular genus of his property i.e "one-third of my estate". It exists at the time of his death. The beneficiary of a general will is entitled to the stated fraction of the property as it exists at the time of the testator's death.[14]

While a specific will is one in which the gift of a particular item of property is distinguished from other property of the same kind - i.e. "my law books." Also, it consists of a share in a particular item of property or a species of property i.e. "one fourth of Rams". It may refer to the testator's property at the time of the bequest and the beneficiary is entitled to the stated fraction of the property as it exists at the time of the bequest.[15]

---

[11] Ibid.

[12] Ibid.

[13] Ibid.

[14] Ibid.

[15] Coulson, N. J. (1964); *Succession in Muslim Family*; Edinburgh, pp. 218–219.

(2) Conditional and contingent will

A conditional will is a bequest coupled with a condition which seeks to regulate either the manner in which the property bequeathed shall be enjoyed or the general conduct and activities of the beneficiaries. Where this is so, it will be enforced against the beneficiaries if the conditions are valid; but where they are not the normal doctrine of severance will apply - i.e. the condition will be ignored and the bequest will remain valid.[16]

This type of will, which derogates from the completeness of the grant takes effect as if no condition was attached to it, for the condition is void.[17] For example, A bequeathed his house to B on condition that B does not sell or let it, and that on B's death it will revert to A's heirs, the conditions are void and the legates takes the house as absolute owner. B may use it or alienate it as he sees fit and on his death it will pass to his own heirs or as he otherwise instructs.

While a contingent will is one which is "suspended upon a condition" and is not to become operative unless and until a specified event takes place or a specified condition is fulfilled. As a general rule, a promise to give in future is not generally binding, but it does not apply to will, which by its nature, is a postponed transfer of ownership and which may be revoked by the testator at any time prior to his death. Hence, the general rule is that contingent wills are valid. But according to a version, this type of will is void.[18]

Void and voidable will

A void will is one in which it is expressly devoted to an illegal purpose such as sexual immorality, gambling or for an improper motive. But a voidable will is one which is not void *ab initio*, but is valid only when certain impediment is removed - e.g. when conditions attached to the will are not valid, they are removed and the will is given effect. Also, a will is not void where it is uncertain, because as a general rule wills do

---

[16] Ibid.

[17] Mulla, D.F.; (1955), *Principles of Mohammedan Law*, 18th ed., Calcutta, p. 144.

[18] Ibid.

not fail on that round of ambiguity or uncertainty.[19]

For example, "I bequest a share in my estate..." will be construed as a bequest of an amount equivalent to the lowest fractional entitlement of any of the legal heirs.

Object of making a will

A will is made to achieve the following objectives:[20]

(i) It is a divine institution since its exercise is regulated by the Holy Qur'an.

(ii) It offers to the testator means of modifying to a certain extent the law of succession.

(iii) It enables some of those relatives who are excluded from inheritance to obtain a share in his property and of recognizing the services rendered to him by a stranger, or the devotion to him in the last moments.

Since these are the objects of making a will it should not be exercised to the injury of the lawful heirs. Hence, the reason for the restriction on the power of testamentary disposition possessed by a Muslim to one-third.[21]

Form of will

There is no prescribed or any particular form required for the making of a will. It can be made verbally or by signs so long as it is apparent that the intention of the testator is to make a disposition operative on his death. But, for convenience sake, it is preferable to be in writing, and witnesses called to its oral declaration. This is supported by the Quranic verse thus:

---

[19] Ibid.

[20] See, Higab M; (1983); *Islam is the all Divine Messages in one*, vol. I; I.P.B. Lagos, p. 220

[21] Ibid.

> O ye who believe: when death approaches any of you, (take) witnesses among yourselves when making bequests, two just men of your own (brotherhood) or others from outside if ye are journeying through the earth.[22]

The burden of proving and establishing an oral will is always a very tedious task, which must be proved with the utmost care and precision; and with every circumstance of time and place.[23]

Testator – al-Musi

A testator is one who makes and executes a will in favour of a legatee to take place after the testator's death:[24]

(i) *He must make a valid offer or declaration (oral or written).* This is because a will is simply a contract and therefore, there must be an offer by the testator and acceptance after his death by the legatee.

(ii) *He must be a freeman.* Freedom is regarded as a necessary condition by all the Schools for a testator. The reason, being that, where he is not a free man - i.e., a slave; he is regarded as a property to be inherited by his master. A slave cannot even own a property, not to talk of making a will.

(iii) *He must be sane.* Sanity is also a necessary condition to the making of a valid will. To Hannafi and Shi'a schools – what is required is a mind that comprehends the nature of the testamentary act. In other words, a disposing mind is required.

(iv) He must not only be an adult but one with full legal capacity i.e. person who has the quality of "*rushd*" – (prudent judgement). A person lacking that is said to be under interdiction. The jurists differ on the issue of a person under legal incapacity to make a valid

---

[22] Ch. 5 v. 109.

[23] Gurin, A.M. (1987), ibid., p. 161.

[24] Ibid.

will.[25]

- Maliki and Hambali schools recognize the validity of a will made by a minor who is a *mumayyiz* - i.e. at the age of discriminating or can differentiate between what is good or bad – which is seven (7) years.
- Hannafi school rejected a will made by a minor (*mumayyiz)* equating it with a gratuitous contract.

(v) He must not exceed the legal one-third rule at all. The bequeathable one-third is calculated only on the date of the death of the testator out of his net estate.

(vi) He must not make a will to any of his legal heirs. Where he has done that, it must not exceed the legal one-third and the other heirs must consent to it. Only Shi'a school allows a will to a heir especially if he is incapacitated.

(vii) He must not make a will in favour of anything that is unlawful or forbidden in Islam. For example, a testator is not to bequeath his house for prostitution, to his dog, etc.

Legatee or beneficiary (Musa Lahu)

A will can be made by a Muslim in favour of any person or body capable of holding property, actually or constructively in existence at the time of the disposition.

This is the view of the Hannafi School – that is, the legatee should be in existence at the time of bequest and if he is not alive, the legacy is not valid. But according to some Maliki jurists a will is valid if made in favour of a legatee Know to be dead, in which case the amount will be used to pay off his debts or will be divided among his heirs.[26]

It can even be made to a child in the womb, but the child, must be born alive in order to be entitled to the legacy. If delivered dead, the legacy to the child is void, but if born alive, then dies, the will is lawful and will be distributed among the child's heir.[27]

---

[25] Ibid., pp. 162 – 163

[26] Ibid.

[27] Ibid., p. 165.

It can also be made to a non-Muslim. In fact, this is the only ground under which a non-Muslim relative can benefit from the estate of his Muslim relative. This is as a result of Islamic stance as a religion of recognizing the rights of the individuals regardless of which creed or faith, the individuals may choose to belong to.[28]

All Schools agree to that, except Shafi'i school which regards a will to a non-Muslim as unlawful where he belongs to the *Darul-Harb* (hostile country). But where he does not belong to a hostile country, bequest to a non-Muslim is lawful and valid.[29]

Where the legatee happens to be one of the heirs such a will is invalid. The reason is that it would amount to giving preference to the heir over others, thus defeating the spirit of the Islamic law which has fixed the portion to each of the heirs.

Another reason is that it causes dispute and hatred amongst persons related to one another. Such type of will is valid only when all the other heirs willingly consent to the bequest. In other words, there is the tendency for the heirs to ratify or reject the will *in toto*, or some of them may ratify partially and others may reject partially.[30]

It is a total ratification of a will, when all the legal heirs unanimously ratify the *ultra vires* bequest. For an heir to ratify the bequest, he has to be sane; attain the age of puberty; and must understand the meaning of ratification. By ratifying the bequest, an heir is deemed to have given his consent on his free will. Thus consent is to be given after the death of the testator.[31]

On the other hand, total rejection of a will, arises where all the legal heirs refused to ratify the bequest of the testator in favour of an heir or in excess of one-third to a non-heir. Where the heirs refused to ratify the bequest in excess of one-third, the doctrine of proportionate reduction of the bequest applies in order to reduce the bequest to one-third, the doctrine of proportionate reduction of the bequest applies in order to reduce the bequest to one-third of the property. This is the view of all the Sunni schools. As to how the proportionate reduction will take place, one is simply to multiply the numerators by 3 after finding out the common denominator. Then finally neglect the common

---

[28] Keffi, S.U.D.; (1990), *Some Aspects or Islamic Law of Succession*; Rukhsa Publications, Kano , p. 31.

[29] Gurin, A.M. (1987), ibid., p. 165.

[30] Ibid., p. 169

[31] Ibid., pp. 171-176

denominator and allow the numerators to remain.[32] For example, P dies leaving property and he has bequeathed ¼ to A, ⅓ to B. This is an *ultra vires* bequest,, because it is more than ⅓ of his property, and since the legal heirs refused to ratify it, it has to be reduced to ⅓ of his property by reducing each of the legatee's share proportionately.

A B

¼ $^1/_3$

$$\frac{3 \qquad 4}{12} = {}^7/_{12}$$

7 x 3 = 21. This shows that the whole property left by P is $^{21}/_{21}$. His bequests will have to be reduced to 1/3 of the property which is = $^7/_{21}$ i.e. A = will now have $^3/_{21}$, B = $^4/_{21}$

The remaining $^{14}/_{21}$ of the property will be distributed to his legal heirs – accordingly.

But partial ratification of a will arises where some of the heirs ratified an *ultra vires* bequest while others refused. The heirs that refused to ratify the will; get their anticipated share according to the rules of intestate succession. While those heirs that ratify the will, must always be ready to sacrifice their share to the satisfaction of the amount ratified.[33] For example, P. is survived by his Mother (M); germaine brother (GB) and his germaine sister (GS). He bequeathed $^2/_3$ of his property to his aged mother which was ratified by the germaine brother and rejected by the germaine sister.

M

$\frac{1}{6}$ $\frac{\text{GB} \qquad \text{GS}}{\text{R}}$

= ($^1/_6 + {}^2/_3 = {}^5/_6$) $^1/_3$ of R ($^6/_6 - {}^5/_6$) ($^1/_3$ of R ($^6/_6 - {}^1/_6$)

($^{14}/_6$) = $^2/_3 \times {}^1/_6 = {}^1/_3 \times {}^5/_6$

$^1/_6$ = Mother's Quranic share

= $^3/_{18}$ = $^2/_{18}$ = $^5/_{18}$

32 Ibid.

33 Ibid., p. 179

The total entitlement of the heirs is:

$$\frac{3+2+5}{18} = {}^{10}/_{18}$$

${}^{18}/_{18} - {}^{10}/_{18} = {}^{8}/_{18}$ which is the ratified value therefore, the mother will get her Quranic share of ${}^{3}/_{18}$ plus the ratified value of:

$${}^{8}/_{18} = \frac{3+8}{18} = {}^{11}/_{18}$$

finally, the entitlement of each heir will be thus:

$$M = {}^{11}/_{18} \qquad GB = {}^{2}/_{18} \qquad GS = {}^{5}/_{18} = {}^{18}/_{18} = 1$$

The mother gets the ${}^{2}/_{3}$ bequest which was ratified by the germaine brother plus ${}^{1}/_{6}$ her Quranic share.

The Germaine brother who ratifies the will must be ready to sacrifice his share to the satisfaction of the amount ratified. That is why his share stands at ${}^{2}/_{18}$. While the germaine sister gets ${}^{5}/_{18}$ because she did not ratify the bequest; despite the fact that the doctrine of Ta'asib (agnatisation) suppose to apply between the germaine brother and sister.[34]

A will to a killer is a subject matter of controversy among the schools, even though they are unanimous that a killer (especially where it is intentional) is debarred from inheritance. Maliki and Shafi'i schools treat a will the same as a gift – that since the killer is not prevented from taking a gift from his victim, the killing will not prevent him as a legatee from benefiting from the will made in his favour by his victim.[35]

Hannafi school is of the view that a will is not valid to a person, who causes the death of the testator even unintentionally, be accident or misadventure. The only exception where the will is valid is where the legatee is an infant or an insane person.[36]

Hambali school is of the view that a will made in favour of the killer of the testator by any form of actionable killing becomes void, unless the testator expressly confirms the will. But Shi'a school is of the view that the killing must be intentional to avoid the legacy to the

---

[34] Ibid.

[35] Ibid.

[36] Ibid.

person causing the death.[37]

Subject-matter of a will (Musa bihi)

The subject-matter of a bequest must be in existence at the time of the testator's death; it is not necessary that it should be in existence at the time of the making of the will. It must also be a property which is lawful, transferable, etc. In short, it must have all the attributes of a property in the eyes of the sharia. When that is the case, the corpus of such property can be the subject matter of a legacy.[38]

Also, the usufruct of such a property can be given as a legacy. For example, the usufruct of an existing property for a limited time or the life time of the legatee may be the basis of a legacy.[39]

Revocation of a will

A will validly made, may be revoked by the testator before his death either expressly or impliedly, or by a subsequent will.[40]

It is an express revocation of a will where the testator revokes the bequest in express terms either orally or in writing. But a mere denial will not constitute a revocation of an otherwise valid will.

An implied revocation is one where the testator does an act from which revocation may be inferred. For example, bequest of a piece of land is revoked, if the testator subsequently builds a house upon it.

A will to a person is also revoked by a subsequent will of the same property to another person. But it will not be a revocation where the same property is bequeathed to two different person in the same will, as both persons take equal shares of the property. It is presumed here, that prior bequest is not revoked by the subsequent one.

---

[37] Ibid.

[38] Higab, M. (1983), ibid., p. 222.

[39] Ibid.

[40] Rashid, K.S.; (1979), *Muslim Law*, Eastern Book Company, p. 216.

The lapse of a will

A will validly made is said to have lapsed, where the legatee predeceases the testator. In this case, in the absence of any contrary intention, it will revert back and form part of the testator's estate. The reason for it being so, is that the legatee is not there to accept the will after the testator's death. All jurists are unanimous on this issue, excepting Shi'a school which says the legacy will not revert to the testator, but instead will go to the heirs of the legatee (where he has) unless the testator revokes it. It will only pass to the testator where the legatee has no heirs.[41]

[41] Verma B. R. (1980), *Mohammedan Law;* 5th ed. Delhi Law House, Allahbad, pp. 448-449.

Chapter 6

Intestate succession

There are circumstances when the devolution of property takes place without the intervention of the owner. The situation crises when the owner of such property dies, without specifying how and in what form should his property be distributed. He is deemed to have died intestate. In order to avoid injustice by denying those entitled to inherit and the awkward situation of how one succeed to a deceased's property during the *jahiliyyah* period, the distribution of such property is made by Allah in the Holy Qur'an:

> From what is left by parents and those nearest related there is a share for men and a share for women, whether the property be small or large determinate share.[1]

Definition

Since the law of intestate succession or inheritance in Islamic law prescribes the mode and manner of succession to a deceased Muslim's property, it can be aptly defined thus:

> A science by which persons (heirs) who inherit are distinguished from those who do not; the knowledge also ascertains, (in most cases), the

[1] Holy Qur'an, Ch. 4 v. 7.

> quantum of the shares, each inheritor is entitled to take. It all centres around the estate (Mal) left by a deceased person.[2]

This shows that Islamic law of intestate succession is an embodiment of the deceased person, the estate (property) and the inheritors. All these must be present, otherwise there can be no succession.

Pre-Islamic law relating to succession

Before Islam, the rules relating to succession are as follows:

i) The nearest male relations succeeded to the entire estate of the deceased;

ii) Female relations were excluded;

iii) Descendants were preferred to ascendants and ascendants to collaterals.[3]

iv) Succession generally on whatever ground was restricted to those men of prowess who also cultivated good horsemanship to crush their enemies in defence of the family. That is why minors and females were not eligible to inherit their deceased relatives.[4]

v) An adopted son inherited the whole property of the adopted father where the latter has no children but where he has, the adopted son inherited along with them.

vi) A person inherited the property of another in the event of his death through clientage or military pact.

vii) A husband inherited the whole of his deceased wife's property to the exclusion of the latter's near relatives.

---

[2] Keffi, S.U.D. (1990); *Some Aspects of Islamic Law of Succession;* Rukhsa Publications, Kano; p. 1.

[3] Rashid K. S.: (1979); *Muslim Law*, Easter Book Company, p. 231.

[4] Keffi, S.U.D.: *op. cit.*, pp. IX-X.

These and many more were what obtained before Islam in relation to succession of a deceased property.

But in Islamic law, different rules of inheritance obtain, and because of its excellence, nearly all the modern writers have admired it.[5]

Rumsey in 'Principles and Precedents of Muhammadan Law' has this to say:

> The Muhammadan Law of inheritance comprises beyond question the most refined and elaborate system of rules for the devolution of property that is known to the civilized world.[6]

Also, Tyabji Kamila in "Limited Interests in Muhammadan Law" said:

> The Muslim law of inheritance has always been admired for its completeness as well as the success with which it has achieved the ambitious aim of providing not merely for the selection of a single individual or homogeneous group of individuals, on whom the estate of the deceased should devolve by universal succession, but for adjusting the competitive claims of all the nearest relations.[7]

Constituents of succession (*Arkanul – Mirath*)

From the definition of succession above, it shows that for succession to take place, there must be the following:

a) The deceased (praepositus);
b) The estate (property); and
c) The heirs or beneficiaries

---

[5] Rashid K. S.: *op. cit.*, p. 229

[6] Ibid.

[7] Ibid.

A deceased person is one who is no longer living in this world and for the sake of succession is a dead person whose assets are transferred to his legal heirs according to the rules of intestate succession depending on the relationship existing between them. All the jurists are unanimous on this, that the death of the deceased is a necessary condition in the law of succession. This death can either be death-in-fact or death-in-law.[8]

There must be, in addition to the death of the praepositus, estate or property left by him, which must be solvent property. It is even the subject-matter of intestate succession. The property may be cash, real property (immovable) property like a car. It can even be the usufruct, i.e. tenancy or trust; rights involving financial obligations not personal right (as in the case of a rank); easement; mortgage; pre-emption, etc.

All the schools excepting Hannafis, agree to all of the above, as inheritable property. But Hannafi school – said only property (real or movable) is inheritable property.

Lastly, there must be heirs as beneficiaries of the property left by the deceased person. These heirs are categorized under blood or marriage, etc.[9]

In addition, the heir or beneficiary, who is a claimant must not be excluded by existence of any preferable heir and there is no impediment to succession. For example, a son is never excluded and should be a Muslim, for it, he is a non-Muslim he cannot inherit the deceased.

The nearer in degree excludes the more remote. For example, a father excludes father's father, or a son excludes son's son, etc.

The strength of consanguinity determines preference. For example, a relation who is related to the deceased through father and mother - i.e. germaine brother - takes preference over a relation who is related to the deceased through the father only - i.e., consanguine brother.

Also, as a general rule, the male heir takes double the portion of a female heir of the same degree. This is based on the Quranic verse saying:

> ...to the male, a portion equal to that of two females.[10]

---

[8] Keffi, S.U.D.: *op. cit.*, pp. 1-3

[9] Ibid.

[10] Ch. 4 v. 11.

The reason for his is that the female have lesser responsibilities and obligations in comparison with the males. Another reason is that man is generally recognized as the bread-winner of the family and this justifies his having greater share than the woman. This position is assigned to him by the Holy Qur'an:

> Men are the protectors and maintainers of women, because God Has given the one more (strength) than the other, and because they support them from their means.[11]

Grounds of inheritance

Before any person inherits from another's property, he must have a connection or relationship with the praepositus. The reasons or causes for this connection are the subject of discussion here. Therefore, any claim of inheritance will only arise when one falls within the following:

i) *Nasab* (blood relationship or tie). The general view is that relatives are grouped into four:

   a) Descendants group take preference in inheritance. Under this group, all direct descendants (whether male or female) can inherit - i.e. son and daughter.
   b) Also, all those connected through the male of direct descendants - i.e. son's son, son's daughter how low soever (h.l.s.).
   c) Ascendants who are directly connected with the deceased or ascendants of direct ascendants - e.g. father and mother or father's father and mother's mother, how high soever (h.h.s.).
   d) Collaterals - i.e. brothers and sisters. As a general rule, all brothers and sisters of all types will inherit - i.e. germaine brothers and sisters (who are of the same mother and father); consanguines (who are of the same father only) and uterines (who are of the same mother only). Also, all male issues of germaines and consanguines inherit in order of priority.
   e) Uncles: on the condition that the claimant is a male and all his male issues will inherit through the deceased e.g. paternal

[11] Ch. 4. 34

uncles, germaine and consanguine and their male issues.

ii) *Nikah* (Marriage)

For marriage to be a ground of inheritance there must be a valid and subsisting marriage at the time of the death. This is the view of all the schools, but as to whether a voidable marriage is a ground of inheritance the schools differ: Hannafi, Shafi'i and Hambali schools said a voidable marriage cannot create right of inheritance. But Maliki school, on the other hand, has two views:

a) Where the irregularity is in dispute and if one of the parties died before they are separated, such voidable marriage will create the right of inheritance.

b) But where there is no dispute as to the irregularity i.e. marriage to a fifth wife; if one of the parties died before they are separated, such a marriage will not create the right of inheritance. Also, where a divorce has been effected, and as long as it is not an irrevocable one and husband and wife exists, provided she is still serving *iddah* (waiting period). These two grounds of inheritance have been unanimously agreed upon by all the Sunni schools through *ijma.*[12]

Liabilities of the deceased

The property left by the deceased person before it is distributed to the beneficiaries is subject to certain charges. This is based on the Quranic verse saying:

> ...after payment of legacies and debts.[13]

This involves such claims as funeral expenses, wills and debts (secured or ordinary debts). It is only when all these are satisfied, the left-over is then to be divided among the heirs (beneficiaries) of the deceased.

---

[12] Gurin, A.M. (1987) – *An Introduction to Islamic Law of Succession* (Testate/Intestate); (Unpublished) C.I.L.S, Ahmadu Bello University, Zaria, pp. 15-18.

[13] Ch. 4 V. 12.

i) Secured debts

It is the liability imposed on a property which has to be settled before anything else. It may take the form of mortgage or *rahn*. So, if the property of the deceased is being mortgaged, the mortgage has to be redeemed first. This is agreed by all the schools except Hambali School. They said, it is the first thing to be settled before any other thing, because during the lifetime of the praepositus, the mortgagee can ask for foreclosure and sells the mortgaged property. And where the mortgaged property is not worth the money borrowed, can lead the mortgagor to be imprisoned.

But Hambali School is of the opinion that funeral expenses should be the first claim to be settled. The reason is that, burial is the first thing on the plaintiff's death.

ii) Funeral expenses

The three schools - Malikis, Hannafis and Shafi'is - are of the view that funeral expenses come second. The expenses are for shrouds – three ordinary garments for man and five ordinary garments for woman; digging; perfumes; transportation, etc.

iii) Ordinary or unsecured debts

All schools agree that general debts come third. Maliki School does not differentiate between general and death–illness debts provided the claim for debts incurred during death–illness are not suspicious. The criteria in ordinary or secured debts are

a) it must be incurred in health; and
b) it must be proved by the ordinary means of proof - i.e. two adults, sane and competent Muslims.

But Hannafi School differentiates the debts for the purpose of payment into:

a) debts incurred during health;

b) debts contracted partly in health and partly in sickness. For this last one, debts incurred partly in health takes preference over the debts incurred partly in sickness.

The unsecured or ordinary debts will also include debts admitted by the praepositus during the death sickness. That is why Maliki School cautioned that there must be no suspicion.

iv) Wills – Wasiyyah

The next thing to be done is the execution of his will, if he has left any. The legacy is to be paid out of the remaining property after deducting the debt and funeral expenses, but not out of the original assets.[14]

Legal heirs

Heirs are those beneficiaries, whom property of a deceased person is transferred to, by the operation of the law. The heirs are grouped into sharers - i.e. Quranic heirs; *residuaries* and the *distant kindred*. The basis for the grouping is found in the following Quranic verses, thus:

> God (thus) directs you as regards your children's (inheritance) to the male, a portion equal to that of two females: if only daughters, two or more, their share is two- thirds of the inheritance; if only one, her share is a half.[15]

This is as regard children of a deceased, namely son(s) and daughter(s) (h.l.s.).

> For parents, a sixth share of the inheritance to each, if the deceased left children; if no children and the parents are the (only) heirs, the mother has a third; if the deceased left brothers (or

---

[14] Gurin, A.M., *op. cit.*, pp. 15-18.

[15] Ibid., Note 40.

> sisters] the mother has a sixth.[16]

This shows the extent to which parents, mother(s) and father(s) (h.h.s.) can inherit to the property of their deceased child:

> In what your wives leave, your share is a half, if they leave no child; but if they leave a child, ye get a fourth...In what ye leave their share is fourth, if ye leave no child; but if ye leave a child, they get an eight...[17]

The above verse, discusses the shares of spouse relics, i.e. husband or wife.

> If the man or woman whose inheritance is in question has left neither ascendants nor descendants; but has left a brother or a sister, each one of the two gets a sixth; but if more than two they share in a third;...[18]

The above verse, discusses the situation when a person dies as a *kalala* a person who dies leaving neither ascendants nor descendants. Collaterals will inherit and from the way the Holy Qur'an has assigned the shares it is understood that they are the *uterine relations* - i.e. those related to the deceased through the mother only.

Also, from the above verse, in relation to the uterines there are three things:

a) Under Islamic law, for one to inherit he has to be related to the deceased through a male issue but uterines are allowed to inherit through a female issue - i.e. the mother.
b) No heir inherits in the presence of the link through which he is inheriting the deceased. But the mother and her children inherit together and neither of them excludes the other.

c) The rule of *Ta'asib* – agnatisation is applicable to those heirs who

---

16 Ibid.
17 Ibid.
18 Ibid.

are related to the deceased in the same degree of relation and removal. That is the male gets twice what the female will get. But it is not applicable to the uterines (male or female), instead they share equally:

> They ask thee for a legal decision say: God directs (thus) about those who leave no descendants or ascendants as heirs. If it is a man that dies, leaving a sister but no child, she shall have half the inheritance; if (such a deceased was) a woman, who left no child, her brother takes her inheritance: If there are two sisters, they shall have two - thirds of the inheritance (between them): if there are brothers and sisters, (they share), the male having twice the share of the female.[19]

The above verse discusses the shares of the collaterals i.e. the agnates; that is the Germaines and consanguine brothers and sisters respectively.

Based on this premise, the heirs can aptly be grouped in to:

a) Sharers or Quranic heirs

They have a fixed share in the estate and this is contained in the Holy Qur'an, *Sunnah* and *Ijma*. This shows that a sharer does not necessary have to be mentioned in the Holy Qur'an alone. For example, mother's mother is a sharer by virtue of the *Sunnah* and a son's daughter by virtue of *Ijma*.

Therefore, the male sharers are:

i) Husband

ii) Father, even though he may inherit as a residuary in addition to his fixed share where he co-exist with a female child or as a residuary where he succeeds alone.

iii) Uterine brother.

---

[19] Ch. 4 v. 176.

While the female sharers are:

i) Wife
ii) Mother
iii) True grandmother (h.h.s.)
iv) Daughter, but may be converted into a residuary heir by the presence of a son
v) Son's daughter (h.l.s.) even though may be converted into a residuary heir by the presence or a son's son.
vi) Germaine sister
vii) Consanguine sister
viii) Uterine sister.

b) Residuaries

They have no fixed shares but who succeed to the residue of the estate after the sharers take their fixed shares.

The residuaries have been divided into three classes, namely:

i) *Residuary in his own right.*

A residuary in his own right is every male in whose line of descent to the deceased no female intervenes - e.g. son, son's son (h.l.s.), father, father's father (h.h.s.), germaine brother and consanguine brother with their sons (h.l.s.), uncle and his sons (h.l.s.).

ii) *Residuary by another*

A residuary in other's right is a female who becomes a residuary only when she co-exist with a male of the same degree - e.g. daughter, son's daughter, germaine sister, consanguine sister co-existing with son, son's son, germaine brother, consanguine brother respectively.

iii) *Residuary with another.*

A residuary with another is a female who becomes a residuary in the presence of another female - e.g. a daughter or son's daughter coming with full sisters or consanguine sisters. The daughter or son's daughter takes her share (½) and the remainder goes to the sisters.

c) Distant kindred (Dhawul-arham)

They are those heirs who are blood relations, but not included in the sharers or residuaries and inherit only when there are no residuaries. In other words, they are heirs in whose line of descent a female intervenes between them and the deceased.

Their position as to whether they can inherit is a subject-matter of disputes among the schools. Maliki and Shafi'i schools are of the view that distant kindred are not to inherit, instead *Bait al-Mal*-Public treasury, takes preference as a legal heir, in the absence of residuary heirs. But in the absence of a properly administered *Bait al-Mal*, the *dhawul-arham* inherit. While Hannafi and Hambali schools – *Bait al-Mal* should not be given the legal status of an heir, instead distant kindred should inherit. They based their view on the premise that he who has strong relationship between the praepositus and himself, logically, should be allowed to inherit, because of two links: Islam and blood relationship. Also, that *Bait al-mal* should not be more than a place for money keeping by giving it the legal status of an heir. Bait al-mal should be a last resort and will inherit as an escheat. Examples of distant kindreds are daughter's daughter, false grandfather or mother, maternal uncles, etc.

(d) Unrelated successors

They are those persons who are entitled to succeed in default of all relations - i.e. universal legatee, acknowledged kinsman. This class of heirs is added by the Hannafi and Shafi'i jurists. Also, *Bait al-Mal* is included here, although, Maliki jurists did not agree with distant kindred and unrelated successors as heirs. Instead, *Bait-al- Mal* is the third after Quranic and residuary heirs.[20]

---

[20] Gurin, A.M.; *op. cit.*, pp. 65-78.

The fractions in succession

There are different types of fractions as far as the shares are concerned; namely:

(i) ½ - a half

(ii) $^1/_3$ - a third

(iii) ¼ - a fourth

(iv) $^1/_6$ - a sixth

(v) $^1/_8$ - one-eight, and

(vi) $^2/_3$ - two-third.

A careful examination of these fractions will lead to three possibilities namely:

(a) either they add up together to get unity; or

(b) to get more than unity; or

(c) to get less than unit.[21]

The circumstances under which and when an heir will get either or these fractions will not be discussed here, for reference has already been made to the famous verses of inheritance - i.e. Chapter 4 v. 11, 12 and 176.

There is no problem whatsoever, when in a given situation of inheritance, the fractions are equal to unity. For example, A dies leaving father, mother and two daughters. The solution will come to *unity*.

---

[21] Ibid.; pp. 142-156.

Example:

	P	
F	M	2D
$^1/_6$ +R	$^1/_6$	$^2/_3$

LCM = 6 = 1 + 0 + 1 + (4) = 6

The problem lies with the situations when the addition is more or less than *unity*.

It will be more than unity and known as ‘AWL i.e. increase, where on allotting the shares to different sharers, it is found that the sum-total of the shares exceeds *unity*. In this case, the share of each sharer shall be proportionately reduced.

For example, if P dies leaving his wife, 2 daughters and his parents.

	W	2D	M	F		
	$^1/_8$	$^2/_3$	$^1/_6$	$^1/_6$ + R		
LCM	3 +	(16) +	4 +	4 + 0 = 27		
		24				
	$^3/_{27}$	$^{16}/_{27}$	$^4/_{27}$	$^4/_{27}$	=	$^{27}/_{27}$

= $^1/_8$ of wife becomes $^1/_9$.

It will be less than *unity* and known as *radd* - i.e., return - where in a situation after allotment, there is a residue. It should be distributed to the sharers in proportions to their shares. The only exception where a sharer is not participating in *radd* is when it involves a spouse relic - i.e., husband or wife. Even then the spouse relic will be entitled to the “return” in default of other sharers or distant kindred.

For example, where P dies leaving a daughter and a mother.

	P	
D	M	
½	$^1/_6$	

LCM $\frac{3 + 1}{6}$ = $^4/_6$

The surplus (two) should be distributed to each heir in proportion to their ½ and $^1/_6$ i.e.

D	=	will be $^3/_4$ instead of $^3/_6$ or ½
M	=	will be $^1/_4$ instead of $^1/_6$

Chapter 7

Legal impediments to acquisition of property

Introduction

The acquisition of property, especially through private ownership is well enshrined in Islam. That is the recognition of man to seek the means of his livelihood on earth according to his capacity, ability and natural endowments. The right to adopt such means in the acquisition as would lead to his moral degradation or upset the social order never accords to him.

Hence, Islam sets up the distinction between *halal* (lawful) and *haram* (unlawful) in respect of the different means of such acquisition and imposes the ban of illegality on all those methods which are morally injurious and styled the unlawful; i.e. bribery, stealing, fraud, deceit, hoarding etc.

Thus, the unlawful means of acquisition can be best termed as the present socio-economic evils. Evil in the economic system begins when the natural selfishness of man exceeds the limits of moderation. It develops with the aid of certain other immoral habits and receives further support from an inherently defective political system, especially if the latter has no moral basis.

After throwing the whole economic system out of gear, it poisons the whole of social life in all its ramifications. Both individual or private ownership of property and the fact of some individuals being economically better placed than others are in accordance with the natural scheme of things and are no evils by themselves. No evil effect could arise from them, if, externally, a political system existed which would maintain justice at all costs, even if it comes to the application of force.

The property acquired or to be acquired by an individual is to be used in such a way as to avoid it being prejudicial to other's property or the interests of the community. The individual is also to avoid or forbidden to have recourse to the exercise in his transactions of such means as fraud, monopoly, usury etc or other disguised transactions that commonly lurk behind the present means of developing wealth in contemporary material civilisation. This has been succinctly summarised by the prophetic saying thus:

> There shall be no damage and no mutual infliction of damage in Islam.[1]

Therefore, the means of acquiring and disposing ownership of property which impedes their legal efficacy are the subject of discussions in this chapter.

Fraud (Gish/Ghabn)

Fraud is defined as a *criminal deception* and perceivable from widely general sense. Muslims are forbidden from committing fraud in their transactions, as the Holy Prophet (S.A.W) is reported to have said:

> He is not one of us who commits fraud.[2]

The Qur'an, has condemned in no uncertain terms those who commit fraud. For instance, Allah the most High says:

> Woe to those that deal in fraud, those who, when they have to receive by measure, from men, exact full measure, but when they have to give by

---

[1] Transmitted by Bukhari and Muslim, as quoted by Higab M. (1983), *Islam is the all Divine Messages in one*, Vol. I. I.P.B. Lagos. Nigeria, p. 185

[2] Transmitted by Bukhari, as quoted by Higab M. (1983), ibid., p. 229.

> measure or weight to men, give less than due. Do they not think that they will be called to account? On a mighty Day, a Day when [all] mankind will stand before the Lord of the worlds.[3]

Also, the Holy Prophet (S.A.W) is reported to have said:

> Purchase and sale are subject to free choice. If the 2 parties speak the truth and make manifest their transactions, they shall be blessed, and if they conceal and tell a lie, the blessing of their transactions shall be obliterated.[4]

It can also be committed by other means not necessarily through business transactions as long as it involves an element of deception. This is more conspicuous with regards to the public funds where large-scale frauds are rampant and what follows is the destruction of vital documents, etc.

It is a fraud where in a transaction - i.e. buying and selling - there is a defect in a property and it is not disclosed to a prospective buyer. If there is any defect impairing a property or thing, it must be pointed out to the intending buyer; otherwise, he is deemed dishonest in his dealings and thus the profits acquired are considered unlawful and Hell-fire will be the abode of anyone who has gained such unlawful profits.

Jabir reported Allah's Messenger as sayings:

> Flesh which has grown out of what is unlawful will not enter paradise, but Hell is more fitting for all flesh which has grown out of what is unlawful.[5]

But a different position obtains in English law and that is the doctrine of 'Caveat Emptor' ('Buyer beware'). This means, the seller is not obliged to disclose a defect in any of his property to be sold, and it

---

[3] The Holy Qur'an; Ch. 83 V. 1-6.

[4] Karim, F.A. (1939), *Al-Hadis Mishkat-ul Masabih*, The Book House, Lahore, Book 2, p. 272.

[5] Transmitted by Ahmad Ibn Hambal or Ors, as Quoted by Karim F.A. (1939), ibid, p. 262.

is up to the buyer to make all the efforts he can afford to find out the defect.

There is an emphasis in Islamic law that the seller must disclose any latent defect to an intending buyer and that is why option is given for repudiation in case of such and other reasons. Hence, the idea of speaking the truth as far as the two parties are concerned.

According to Abu Huraira, once, when passing by a grain merchant, the Holy Prophet's curiosity was aroused. He thrust His hand into the heap of grain and found it wet. So, He asked the owner of the grain how that came about. On being told that rain had fallen on it He said:

> Why did you not put the wet part on the top of the grain so that people might see it? He who deceives has nothing to do with Me.[6]

Also, Wathilah narrated that he heard the Holy Prophet (S.A.W.) say:

> If anyone sells a defective article without drawing attention to it, the Angels will continue to curse him.[7]

Therefore, the best thing to observe is the practice of exposing the defects of what one sells, of telling the truth and giving good advice.

Ibn Sirin, when he sold a sheep, he told the buyer:

> I would like to tell you about a defect it has: it kicks the fodder.[8]

Also, when al-Hassan bin Salih, sold a slave girl he told the buyer:

> Once she spat up blood.[9]

---

6 Siddiqi, A.H. (1979). *Sahih Muslim:* Sh. Muhammad Ashraf, Lahore, Pakistan, vol. III, p. 804.

7 Ibid.

8 Al-Qaradawi, Y; (1984); *The Lawful and the Prohibited in Islam:* I.I.F.S.O.: pp. 260-262.

9 Ibid.

These and more of the like are examples of what is required as it pertains to a defect in a property to be sold, even if it will result in receiving a lower price.[10]

Fraud includes the practice of going out to buy property which is on its way to the market. This practice has been prohibited by the Holy Prophet (S.A.W. that one is to wait until it was brought to the market-place. The reason is that there is a possibility of the seller not knowing the current price of his goods, thereby may be defrauded. Where a property is sold in this manner, the seller has the option of cancelling the transaction after arriving at the market place.[11]

It also refers to the manipulation of the market through the practice of what is termed *najash*. Ibn Umar, explained that *najash* signifies someone's bidding for an item in excess of its price without having any intention of actually buying it, but merely in order to induce others to bid still higher. Many times this is pre-arranged for the purpose of defrauding others.[12]

It may also occur in companies, government ministries and parasatals, as when the preparation of the finished goods is in process or when raising vouchers or entrusted with public funds. In short, fraud occurs in almost every profession or occupation, e.g. tailoring, weaving, food, etc. Thus the Holy Prophet (S.A.W) made it known that the fraudulent person is excluded from the meaning of the expression:

> People of Religion (*Din*) and faith (*Iman*) just as He said a thief and wine-drinker cannot be believers.[13]

Hoarding (*Ihtikar*)

Hoarding is also known as *idle wealth*. It is defined as the withholding of property in use in order to raise their prices artificially.

In any given business, there is the aim of profit making as its sole objective. One is to put the property in the market, sell it for a reasonable profit, buy more of the property and sell them in like

---

[10] Ibid.

[11] Ibid.

[12] Ibid.

[13] Ibn Taymiya; (1982); *Public Duties in Islam. The Institution of Hisba*; The Islamic Foundation; pp. 29-33.

manner and so on. This practice serves the public interest. Anyone who acquires and disposes property through this practice is both blessed and well provided for by Allah. The Holy Prophet (S.A.W) is reported to have said:

> He who brings goods to the market is blessed with bounty...[14]

The other way of not allowing property to circulate in the market is to withhold the property from the market until it becomes scarce and those who need it are unable to find it, then compelled by their need, they come to the hoarder and pay him the price he demands, although it may be unreasonably high. This practice is known as hoarding.

A market place in a typical Islamic setting is one in which it prevails the freedom for an individual and the natural competition devoid of ambition, greed, and selfishness, accumulative tendency to property at the expense of others, and enriching oneself by the manipulation of prices of property.

This is why the Holy Prophet (S.A.W.) denounced hoarding and hoarders in very strong terms thus:

> ...but he who withholds them is cursed.[15]

Also, He said:

> If anyone withholds goods until the price rises, he is a Sinner.[16]

Hoarding has the effect of inflicting injury to the people by the hoarder's sinister motive of forcing the price up in order to make more profit.

---

[14] Khan, M.M. (1976) *Sahih al- Bukhari;* Hilal Yayinlari, Ankara-Turkey, Vol.III, p. 186.

[15] Karim, F.A. (1939), Ibid, Book II, p. 265.

[16] Siddiqi, A.H. (1976), Ibid, Vol. III, p. 845.

Bribery (*Rashwah*)

Muslims are allowed or permitted to acquire property as much as they desire, as long as they acquire it through the lawful means and increases such property through lawful investments only. Taking a bribe is one way out of many ways of acquiring property wrongfully and unlawfully.

A bribe is then defined as any kind of property which is offered to a judge, public servant, a person in authority against a rival, to expedite one's own affair, or to delay that of one's competitor, etc.

Islam has prohibited the offering and accepting or bribery as stated in the Holy Qur'an thus:

> And do not eat up your property among yourselves for vanities; nor use it as bait for the judges, with intent that ye may eat up wrongfully, and knowingly a little of (other) people's property.[17]

The Holy Prophet (S.A.W.) said:

> Allah's curse is on the one who offers the bribe, the one who receives it, and the one who arranges it.[18]

From the above Quranic verse; it is not allowed for one to use his own property for corrupting others in the form of bribery to judges, persons in authority, etc.

Bribery and corruption has many facets to it and the following incidents during the time of the Holy Prophet (S.A.W.) are examples of it:

1. The Holy Prophet (S.A.W) sent 'Abdullah bin Rawahah to the Jews to estimate what they owed as taxes on their palm trees. The Jews offered him some money as a gift. He said to them "what you have offered as a bribe is *haram* (unlawful) and we do not accept it.[19]

---

[17] Ch. 2 v. 188.

[18] Karim, F.A. (1939), ibid., Book I, p. 523.

[19] Transmitted by Bukhari and Muslim, as quoted by Qaradawi Y. (1984), ibid., p. 332.

2. The Holy Prophet (S.A.W) sent a man to collect *zakat* (poor dues) from the Azd tribe. On returning to the Holy Prophet (S.A.W.) he kept something for himself, telling the Holy Prophet thus:

> That is for you and this is for me as a gift.

Thereupon, the Holy Prophet (S.A.W) became angry and said, thus:

> If what you say is right, would these gifts have reached you if you had remained in your father's or your mother's house? He then continued; why should a person employed by me 'say, that this is for you and this is for me as a gift?' Did gifts reach him while he lived in his mother's house? By Him in whose hand is my soul, no one, takes something wrongfully without Allah's making him carry it on the Day of Resurrection, carrying a braying camel, a mooing cow, or a bleating goat (which he received in this manner).[20]

The effect of bribery by its proliferation in a society is that it leads to corruption and oppression allowing the asking of unjust decisions and the just ones are not allowed but blocked, undeserving persons are given chances and deserving ones are by-passed, and the spirit of greed permeates the society in place of the spirit of dutifulness.

The reference to a *bribe as a gift* cannot transform it from *haram* (unlawful) to *halal* (lawful). Therefore, the yardstick to determine whether a person in authority is to receive property as a gift, should imagine himself sitting in his parents' house and thinking that even after leaving the job he will still have received the gift there, then he may accept the gift offered to him. But, if on the other hand, the reverse is the case, he must not accept it.

Death–sickness gift (*Ahwal Mard-ul-Mawt*)

Death-sickness (*Mard-ul-Mawt*) is defined as an illness with proximate

---

[20] Transmitted by Bukhari and Muslim, as quoted by Qaradawi Y. (1984), ibid., p. 332.

danger of death which causes an apprehension of death in the mind of the person suffering from it and which eventually results in such person's death.[21]

Islamic law attached certain particular consequences to acts done during death-illness. The consequences of such illness affects among others, the law relating to transfers i.e. gifts.

The right of a Muslim to make a gift of his property during his death–illness shall be subject to restrictions as those imposed on a testator. That is, it should not be more than a legal one-third and where the gift is to an heir, the consent of other heirs is required.

The reason for prohibiting death–sickness gift is to avoid the unfortunate situation of the beneficiary of such gift having undue advantage, or denying or preventing those entitled to benefit from the property from doing so.

Theft (*Sariqah*)

Theft is the act of taking other people's property without any lawful claim to it. It is also defined as the taking away of property recognised in law as belonging to another from where it is kept and carried it away with the intention of appropriating it with justifying one's actions commits the crime of theft.

Islamic law has recognised and maintained the inviolability of property. It has provided means of acquiring such property once they are lawful. Its transfer also, has to be according to law.

Acquisition of property by individual, whether male or female, is recognised as one of the basic laws regulating human society. All unlawful means of acquiring property are denounced.

> And do not eat up your property among yourselves for vanities, nor use it as bait for the judges, with intent that ye may eat up wrongfully and knowingly a little of (other) people's property.[22]

Therefore, theft, among others, is punishable crime and prohibited as being false or dishonest means of acquiring property. The reason,

---

[21] B.R. Verma's; (1980); *Mohammedan Law*; Delhi Law House; p. 760.

[22] Ch. 2 v. 188.

being, it promotes the habits of indolence thereby negating honest labour and reducing some members of the society to penury while others prosper at their expense.

In order to protect the sanctity and inviolability of property, the Holy Qur'an provides measures to be taken where it is not maintained.

> As to the thief, male or female, cut off his or her hands; a punishment by way of example, from God, for their crime; and God is Exalted in power.[23]

This has been supported by a prophetic tradition where it was reported by Aisha that a thief was brought to Allah's Messenger and He had his hand cut off. Those who brought him said: 'We did not think you would go as far as this with him.' He replied:

> By God, if Fatima, daughter of Muhammad had been the one, I would have had her hand cut off.[24]

To further protect the property, it is provided that even after the punishment, it should be returned. All the jurists have agreed that the thief if punished by *hadd* (prescribed punishment) for the crime of theft, is also liable to deliver the stolen property to its rightful owner if it is physically in the possession of such thief, or could be traced in any transaction. This has been based on the authority of the *hadith* that:

> Whoever finds his own property in the unlawful possession of another person could redeem it.[25]

Based on the above *hadith*, the jurists of the Sunni schools are divided, as to how the property should be redeemed.

Imam Malik is of the view that the thief in addition to the *hadd* punishment, is liable to pay damages (*daman*) if the stolen property had perished or is being consumed provided that he is in a good financial position from the date of committing the theft to the date of punishment by the *hadd*. But if he is destitute no damages lies against him and it is

---

[23] Ch. 5 v. 41

[24] Karim, F.A. (1939), Ibid, Book 2, p. 559.

[25] Transmitted by Abu Dawud in Sunnan Vol. 3; p. 3531.

immaterial if he gets rich after the date of punishment.[26]

Imam Abu Hanifa is of the view that no damages will be paid by the thief convicted of the *hadd* of theft, if the stolen property had perished, or was consumed, because *hadd* and damages could not be combined in such circumstance. The thief is to deliver the stolen property to the owner if the property materially exists or is traceable. He reserved that if the stolen property had perished or was consumed and the *hadd* punishment was not inflicted due to some reasonable doubt (*shubha*), the thief is liable to damages or restitution.[27]

But Imams Shafi'i and Hambali are of the view that if the stolen property could not be redeemed as in the case of perishable or consumed goods, the thief is liable to restitute the stolen property or pay adequate damages for its market value on the date of theft.[28]

Impediments to inheritance (*Mawani'al-Irth*)

Because of the importance attached to property and inheritance as a means for acquiring private ownership of such property, the law relating to it, is specified in the Holy Qu'ran.[29] The sharers to partake in the inheritance have been spelt out. This shows the distribution of property is being done by the Holy Qur'an; and expressed by the Holy Prophet thus:

> Give the fixed portions to those who are entitled to them; and what remains should go to the nearest male.[30]

Based upon the above, any person who is related to the deceased is entitled to inherit, unless there is some legal cause which excludes him, and the most important of these, are subject of discussion. The reason being, they impede the acquisition (or transferring) of the ownership of property.

---

[26] Ibn Asim; Mayyaras – Commentary on Tuhfa, p. 268.

[27] Al-Sarkhasi; *al-Mabsout*; Vol. 9; p. 176.

[28] Ibn Qudamah; *al-Mughni*; Vol. 10; p. 279.

[29] Ch. 4 v. 11, 12 and 176, Known as the three fundamental verses on inheritance.

[30] Siddiqi, A.H. (1976), ibid., Vol. III, p. 852.

[a] Difference of religion

Even, where an heir and the deceased are related, the heir cannot inherit the deceased if they are of different religions. All Muslim jurists unanimously agreed on this point. This is based on the Quranic verse saying:

> And never will God grant to the unbelievers away (to triumph) over the believers.[31]

There are a lot of *hadith* reported from the Holy Prophet (S.A.W.) to that effect. One of which is thus:

> A Muslim cannot inherit from the non-Muslim and non-Muslim cannot inherit from the Muslim.[32]

An exception from this rule is stated by Mu'awiyyah, Mu'adh b. Jabal, Ibn Musayyib and others, followed by Shi'a schools who allow a Muslim to inherit his non-Muslim relative, while a non-Muslim relative is not allowed to inherit a Muslim.[33] Their reason for so doing might not be unconnected with the verse saying:

> And never will God grant to the unbelievers a way (to triumph) over the believers.[34]

This shows that the Muslims should always have the upper hand as against the non-Muslims; hence their justification for allowing a Muslim to inherit his non-Muslim relative.

(b) Apostasy-(Riddah)

Apostasy is the renunciation or abandonment of Islam by one who professes the Islamic faith and to be received into the faith of the

---

[31] Ch. 4 v. 141.

[32] Siddiqi, A.H. (1976), ibid., Vol. III , p. 852.

[33] Siddiqi, A.H. (1976), ibid., Vol. III , p. 852.

[34] Ch. 4 v. 141

unbelievers.[35]

Any person who has willingly abandoned Islam is not entitled to inherit at all, whatever his relationship with the deceased might be. This is the view of all the schools. The Muslim relative will not inherit the apostate also. The prohibition operates in both sides - i.e. as a double-edged sword. This is based on a prophetic tradition thus:

> Muslims do not inherit from non-Muslims.[36]

As to what happens to an apostate's estate, the schools are divided, especially Maliki and Hannafi schools. Maliki School is of the view that the apostate's estate or property will be inherited by *Bait al-Mal* or public treasury. Hannafi school is of the view that the apostate's estate or property acquired before apostasy will be inherited by his heirs and the ones acquired after apostasy will be inherited by the public treasury.

(c) Homicide

Homicide, which is killing can be either intentional or unintentional. This categorisation is important because of the Quranic verse which says:

> Never should a Believer kill a Believer; but (if it so happens) by mistake, (Compensation is due)...If a man kills a Believer intentionally, his recompense is Hell, to abide therein (forever).[37]

Where the killing is intentional, the killer is not allowed to inherit whatever his relationship with the deceased might be. The reason is two-fold:[38]

1) In order to prevent universal disorder which is bound to happen in a

---

[35] Rahman, S.A; (1978); *Punishment of Apostasy in Islam*; Institute of Islamic Culture, Lahore , Pakistan

[36] Gurin, A.M. (1987), ibid., p. 45.

[37] Ch. 4 v. 92-93

[38] Keffi, S.U.D. (1990); *Some Aspects of Islamic Law of Succession;* Rukhsa Publications, Kano; pp. 29-30.

Muslim society, since the accused as heir will be tempted to accelerate the death of his victim/relative in order to inherit.

2) To stop a criminal i.e. the killer, from taking the advantage of the crime he has committed.

But, where it is unintentional killing, the killer is not prevented from inheriting the deceased if he is an heir. The only exception is that the killer will not inherit from *Diyyah* - i.e. blood money, payable to the relatives of the deceased, even if he happens to be one of them.[39]

(d) Slavery

Slavery is a condition of being a slave and a slave is a person who is the property of another and bound to serve him. A slave is not entitled to inherit from a free man. This is the view of all the Sunni and Shi'a schools. Slavery in Islamic law is either *perfect and absolute*, as when the slave and all that he possesses are wholly at the disposal of his master; or *imperfect and privileged*, as when the master has promised the slave his freedom on his paying a certain sum of money by easy instalments, or, without any payment after the death of the master.[40]

The reason why a slave is not allowed to inherit might not be unconnected with economic factors, i.e. did not own freedom, cannot acquire property and consequently cannot inherit.

---

[39] Ibid., p. 24

[40] Gurin, A.M.; (1987), ibid., 41

Index

www.ingramcontent.com/pod-product-compliance
Lightning Source LLC
Chambersburg PA
CBHW031328230926
51848CB00001B/144